# WAKE UP!

GOD'S PROPHETIC

CALENDAR IN

TIMELINES AND FEASTS

**Wake Up!**
**God's Prophetic Calendar in Timelines and Feasts**

Originally printed in Dutch: January 2014
Copyright © (Arno Lamm & Emile-Andre Vanbeckevoort), 2017
Published by: Branchpress, United Kingdom

Cover Design: Willem van Veelen
Typesetting: TM Graphics
Printed by Page Bros, Norwich

**ISBN-13: 978-0-9528865-3-2**
Website book: www.wakeup.community

**Concise Edition**

'Special thanks to John Wright of Branch Press for making this concise edition of WAKE UP available.'

For other titles from Branch Press visit
www.branchpress.com

# Content

**Chapter One**

# INTRODUCTION

There is often a general belief in the return of Jesus Christ without any expectation of his coming in our time. This book is not to defend any particular belief, but to help the Bride of Christ to be watchful and prepare for the coming of the Bridegroom.

An understanding of the Biblical Feasts and the ancient Jewish wedding ceremony is essential for Christians to understand the words of Jesus about the last days. We need to recognise that the Biblical Feasts reflect the Christian life and pay especial attention to the time of the last harvest in the autumn, which is also called the wedding season.

God told Daniel that in the last days the wise would be able to understand the prophecies. There are still too many neglecting the need of the Bride of Christ to have a daily life prepared for His return. How can a bride afford to be unready for the wedding?

Of course the Institutional Church has always included weeds and wheat. But when the Bride of Christ is mentioned, it is not about a religious qualification. It refers to those who have had an internal change of heart and who manifest an external walk of faith. Those who have been born again and are led by the Spirit.

After the taking away of the Bride, also known as the rapture, there will still be "churches" on earth, but they will be deceived. While a substantial number will repent, many others will have become part of the new world order of the Antichrist led by the False Prophet.

# Chapter Two

# GOD'S PLAN INTERWOVEN IN THE OLD TESTAMENT

Many Christians think that the Old Testament is less relevant to them, since they are believers of the New Testament. Some even think that only the Pauline epistles apply to Christians. But the Old Testament is not just about the Old Covenant, and the New Testament is not just about the New Covenant. Christ is manifest from the start of the Old Testament as is the certainty of God's pre-ordained plan for His creation.

The Hebrew Language is both *phonetic* like western languages, transferred by sound, but also *pictographic* by which letters and words can have several levels of meaning.

Jesus said that the mysteries behind parables would be revealed to those who really want to 'know the secrets of the kingdom.'[1] If we adopt the Hebrew perspective we will discover four levels of interpretation:

1. **Peshat** - direct, simple interpretation. If this does not fit, search for the meaning at the next level.

2. **Remez** - a hint or veiled allusion. Example: when God gave orders how to respond to a knocked out tooth or a damaged eye, it meant the whole body.

3. **Derash** - requiring a search to unravel. Example: when Joseph & Mary fled to Egypt, it was to fulfil Hosea's word, *'Out of Egypt I have called my Son.'* These Bible texts need each other to be explained.

4. **Sod** - a hidden message. Example: Paul talks about mysteries in **Romans**[2] and John speaks of the mystery of 666[3].

God chose the Hebrew language to instruct His people, but the so-called Old Testament has been translated in Greek, bringing possible confusion from two different mind-sets. The disciples came together[4] on the

---

1  Matt. 13:10-17.
2  Rom. 11:25.
3  Rev. 13:16.
4  Acts 20:7.

'first day of the week'. That is what one would read not knowing the Hebrew context of the Feasts. But in the Greek New Testament the word for 'week' is plural and should be translated as 'weeks'. A Hebrew mind-set would realise that this was the first (day) of the seven weeks up to Pentecost. That adds a totally different dimension to this meeting of the disciples.

God gave Moses the written Torah, the first five books of the Bible, and this was followed by the Oral Instruction, interpretations given by Moses to the seventy elders. These instructions were handed down through generations. Jesus said that people should listen to Moses as taught by the Pharisees, but not their unscriptural burdens, including those they did not practice themselves!

At the Reformation the principle of 'Sola Scriptura' – the scripture of the Bible alone – was established. The Bible was the only theological source and was also a protection against Roman Catholic rituals. As a result, there has also been a tendency to reject the complete Oral Instruction and the written Talmud to avoid legalism.

But Jesus often taught from the Oral Instruction, as on the question of divorce, and He celebrated the Chanukah Feast in the Temple even though this feast was not "Scriptura" based, but celebrated the re-dedication of the Second Temple in 165 BC.

Sola Scriptura needs therefore to exercise discernment in accepting from the Jewish traditions in the Oral Instruction and the Talmud only those things that are confirmed by the Bible as being of divine origin. But with this biblical filter these are well worth studying.

Another problem arises when postmodern scholars want to interpret the Bible to fit in with the values of society today. In Israel it was the other way round. Each generation was called to adjust its values and behaviour to the Biblical norm. In every generation the broad highway that leads to destruction is very attractive and needs to be retuned with the truth of the Bible!

Understanding the Bible requires three main ingredients. **First** we need to refer to the original Hebrew or Greek language. **Secondly** we have to interpret texts with knowledge of Hebrew culture. **Thirdly** we have to be aware that some texts, such as the parables, have meanings at several levels, some of which are hidden or need seeking out.

For example, some believe the seven churches in Revelation are what existed at the time – **Peshat**; others believe they represent (and are hints of) consecutive periods of church history - **Remez**; others believe these churches are types that will co-exist in the end times – **Derash**. All levels are possible.

Like the Talmud, Christian translations of the Bible suffer from human bias and error. Talking about the "Jewish" feasts, according to some translations Paul writes , *'They are only a shadow of things that were going to come.'*[1] The original text does not have, *'only'*, and they are actually shadows or types of, *'what is to come'*. They refer not only to the first coming of Christ, but also to His return.

The Old Testament shadows (types) help us to see Christ revealed in such stories as the wedding of Ruth (representing the Gentiles) and Boaz (the kinsman redeemer and a type of Christ). Christ appears throughout the Old Testament. He was the priest Melchisedek, the man with the drawn sword before Joshua, the man clothed in linen talking to Daniel, the fourth man in the fiery furnace. As others have already realised, the Old Testament conceals the New Testament and the New Testament reveals the Old Testament.

Jesus described Himself as the Alpha and the Omega, or in Hebrew, the Aleph and Tav, the One Who is, and Who was, and Who is to come.[2] The

---

1  Col. 2:16.
2  Rev. 1:8.

Aleph letter means initiator or author and the Tav letter means finisher. So Paul writes that Jesus is the *'author and the finisher of our faith'*, pointing to the Aleph and Tav.[1] Be aware that in Hebrew, the writing goes from right to left.

Christ is also revealed in the Old Testament in the Hebrew text by the letters Aleph Tav (את).[2] Esau had AT before his name until he gave up his birth right when it passed to Jacob. Ruth had no את before her name until she married Boaz and then she received the את mark of the Redeemer. The untranslated את symbol appears more than 7000 times in the Bible speaking of Jesus Christ.[3]

The disciples judged Jesus Christ to be Messiah, not because of His miracles, but because He conformed to what God had revealed in the Tanakh - the Law, the Writings and the Prophets of the Old Testament. Even so the Jews in Berea were searching the (Old Testament) scriptures daily to see if everything Paul said about Jesus was laid out in the Scriptures.[4]

---

1 Hebr.12:2.
2 Gen. 1:1.
3 There is an extensive study about the Aleph Tav in the unabridged version of Wake Up!
4 Acts 17:11.

# Chapter Three

# GOD'S APPOINTED TIMES

*'Declaring the end from the beginning, and from ancient times things that are not yet done.'* Isaiah 46:10.

## Introduction

Prophecies given up to 25 centuries ago were unexplainable to people at the time, and not very relevant to them. But now we are seeing them come to pass.

But the Christian Church is largely asleep and disconnected from its Old Testament roots. It comforts itself by saying that even Jesus did not know the time of His return, it would be like a thief in the night, and a day is as a 1000 years to God – so we may still have a long time to wait.

The prophet Daniel received an account of the Last Days, but was told that some pieces would be hidden until the end. As he foretold, knowledge and travel have increased enormously. Just look back and see where we were only 100 years ago. In order to better understand the times, we are encouraged to look at seven timelines to see where we are and how close our days are to the return of Jesus Christ.

## 1. One Day is Like 1000 Years

A thousand years are as yesterday in God's sight.[1] Approximately 4000 years have passed from Adam to the crucifixion of Jesus Christ. Since then two thousand years have passed and the Bible says one thousand years of peace (God's Great Sabbath) will follow to complete the seven thousand year time frame appointed to mankind. These reflect the seven days of the Creation week.

The prophet Hosea said that after two days God would revive Israel and on the third day God would raise them up. Many believe that the two days started at the time of Jesus' coming to Israel and will be ending in the Millennium, which is then the third day of thousand years. This belief in seven thousand years was also held by Rabbi Elijah two hundred years before Christ, and by the early Church.

---

1  Ps. 90:4 & 2 Peter 3:8.

One problem is that 2017 was the year 5777 on the Hebrew Calendar and the question is: does this mean we are 223 years away from the return of Messiah? We need to realise that this calendar was drawn up by Rabbi Yose ben Halafta in the second century. His teacher was Rabbi Akiva who had pronounced Simon bar Kokhbar to be Messiah. So adjustments were made to the Jewish calendar to confirm this. Unfortunately they trusted in a false messiah and in 135 AD 580,000 Jews were killed by the Romans. The remainder were dispersed throughout the earth until the prophesied time of God's forgiveness in response to Israel's repentance would come.[1]

### 2. The Image of Nebuchadnezzar and the Times

Nebuchadnezzar had a dream that only Daniel was able to interpret with God's help.[2] The king had seen a statue made of four metals – a head of Gold, then other parts of Silver, Brass and Iron. Daniel explained that these metals foretold empires that would follow the king who himself was shown as the golden head. Looking back on history we can see that the Medes and Persians were silver, the brass was Greece, the iron was and is Rome and iron and clay is the last world order empire. Finally the king saw a stone not cut by human hands (Christ Jesus) destroy the iron and clay empire and with it all spiritual powers that were behind these previous empires who reigned over all the earth. Daniel was foretold how the future would end.

### 3. The Divisions of 490 years

The historian Frank Paine found that when Jesus commanded us to forgive 'seventy times seven' he was also referring to divine seasons of 10x49 = 490 years. Researchers have found that from Adam to Abraham there were **four** periods of 490 years; from Abraham to Exodus was the **fifth** period; from Exodus to Solomon's Temple was the **sixth** period; from then until the second temple was the **seventh** period; from then until the death of Jesus was an **eighth** period of 490 years; from Jesus to the present day there have been four more periods of 490 years making

1  Hos. 14.
2  Dan. 2.

a total of **twelve** periods. When the fiftieth Jubilee years are added, it comes to 6000 years.

But when Paul talks about *'the purpose of the ages'*[3], he hints that God has a time plan. He not only holds the future, He also divides it into divisions of time.

### 4. Our History in 120 Jubilee Cycles
God says, *'My Spirit shall not always strive with man, for they are flesh: yet his days shall be 120 years.* Genesis 6:3.

As some men and women lived for more than 120 years even after the flood, it could be understood that God will not finally judge mankind before 120 divisions of time are passed. This is generally recognised as 120 Jubilees, because the Hebrew word there can also mean "divisions of time".

God moves time in cycles: One day is the rotation of the earth; one year is the orbit of the earth round the sun. A Sabbath year ends seven years and the Jubilee year ends seven periods of seven years. From Creation to Abraham there were forty Jubilee cycles; from Abraham to Jesus Christ there were forty Jubilees; from Jesus to His return there will be forty Jubilees. So there will be 120 Jubilees before Christ returns to the Mount of Olives. We are now approaching the end of the 120th Jubilee!

### 5. The Seventy Weeks of Years
*'Seventy weeks are determined upon thy people and upon thy holy city, to finish the transgression and to make an end of sins, and to make reconciliation for iniquity, and to bring everlasting righteousness, and to seal up the vision and the prophecy, and to anoint the most holy.'* Daniel 9:24.

God tells Daniel in the following verses that there will be 69 weeks of Years (69 x 7= 483 years) until an anointed One shall be cut off (The crucifixion); after this one more week (7 years) will need to be completed.

---
3   Eph. 3:11.

In the 19th century Sir Robert Anderson, head of criminal investigation at Scotland Yard, worked out that by using the Hebrew calendar of 360 days, there were 173,880 days to complete the 69 weeks. Most historians agree that Artaxerxes gave the command to re-build Jerusalem on 15th March 445 BC. Go forward 173,880 days and we arrive in his calculation at 6th April 32 AD, the day of Jesus's entry into Jerusalem. The remaining 7 years is believed by many to refer to the final seven year tribulation that has still to come, because God said to Daniel that this 70th week will end the period to finish the transgression, and to make an end of sins, and to make reconciliation for iniquity, and to bring in everlasting righteousness.

### 6. The Time Line to the New State of Israel in 1948

God told Ezekiel to lie on his left side for 390 days for the iniquity of Israel and to lie on his right side for 40 days for the iniquity of Judah, making 430 years of punishment.[1] Why this long? In Leviticus God gave the people a choice between blessing or curse. If they would give every seventh year as a Sabbath to the Lord, planting no crops and no harvesting but relying on His provision, they would be blessed. From the time that Saul became king of Israel this command was ignored for 490 years.

After 490 years of not keeping the sabbath for the land every seventh year, God told Israel[2] that they owed Him 70 sabbatical years so the land would be desolate for 70 years, the exact period of the Exile. But in Leviticus[3] God warned that continued disobedience would multiply his punishment seven times. After the Babylonian Exile, 360 of the 430 years of judgement from the vision in Ezekiel[4] were still left. But the people of Israel remained disobedient. So, if the remaining 360 years are multiplied seven times, Israel would not be able to control their land for a further 7 x 360 = 2520 years.

From the return to Jerusalem in 537 BC Chuck Missler multiplied the remaining 360 years in the time of Ezekiel by 7 = 2520 years using the

---

1  Ezek. 4:4-7.
2  Jer. 25:11, 29:10, 2 Chron.36:20-22)
3  Lev.26:18
4  Lev.4:1-6

prophetic calendar. Using the Gregorian calendar this is 2483 years, 9 months and 14 days. So adding this period to 537 BC takes us to the year 1948 – the year of the re-establishment of the sovereign nation of Israel.

In 587 BC the temple and Jerusalem were destroyed by Nebuchadnezzar. 70 years later in 518 BC they were re-built. 2438 years, 9 months and 14 days later takes us to 1967 – the year of the six day war when Israel won back all of Jerusalem.

Daniel saw "Mene, Mene, Tekel, Upharsin" written by God on a wall.[5] These measures amount to 1260 shekels or the equivalent of 2520 geerahs. So God spoke of the 2520 years as the period before God's judgement of Babylon in Revelation 11-13.

It is amazing that there were 2520 years:

- from the start of the Babylonian exile to the first Jewish settlement in 1878.

- from Israel's return from exile to the restoration of Israel in 1948.

- from the re-building of the temple to the recovery of Jerusalem in 1967.

In fact we see an ancient time pattern being mirrored in our time. With all this God has restored the Hebrew language through the efforts of Eliezer ben Yehuda; Ezekiel's dry bones are restored to life and the time is coming when a great army will stand on its feet, filled with His Spirit. Amazing Grace!

### 7. The generation after 1948
What will happen after the re-establishment of the State of Israel? Jesus said it would be, 'the beginning of sorrows.'[6] Although there have always

---

5  Dan. 5:25.
6  Matt. 24:8.

been wars, famines and earthquakes, there has been an enormous increase since this last century.

The Delitisch Hebrew translation of the New Testament suggests that when Jesus said, '*From the fig tree (Israel) learn its lesson. As soon as its branch becomes tender...you know that summer is near*', He was playing a word game, not unusual in Hebrew. Jesus makes the connection of 'summer'[1] with the word 'end'[2] and with the fig tree, Israel. He shows that the summertime (end time) of sorrows[3] will happen when the fig tree has started to blossom.

Soon Jerusalem will become a 'cup of reeling' to her adversaries. [4]
Jesus said that the generation that sees these things will see His return. 70 years is generally considered as a generation, so from 1948 we come to 2018 and from 1967 we come to 2037. We are indeed a few minutes before midnight![5]

Jesus also spoke of signs in the heavens.[6] In 2014 and 2015 there were, back to back, four total lunar eclipses (tetrads) that took place on the feasts of Pesach and Tabernacles. Lunar eclipses as such are not that exceptional, but tetrads are. Jews interpret Tetrads as possible signs of coming trouble and strife. The last tetrad before 2014-15 was in 1967/68 when the Jews recovered Jerusalem. Before that was a tetrad in 1949/50 when the Jews were attacked at the start of the new State of Israel.

The Hebrew people have always seen time as a dynamic and recurrent process. There were seven days in Creation, the seventh being a day of rest for God. There were seven days in a week, the seventh being a day of rest for men. There were seven years of labour, the seventh being a

---

1  Phonetically Kayitz.
2  Phonetically Ketz.
3  Matt. 24:32.
4  Zech.12:2.
5  Matt. 24:34.
6  Gen. 1:14 & Matt.24:29.

year of rest for the land. There are seven days of 1000 years, the seventh bringing Millennial Shalom!

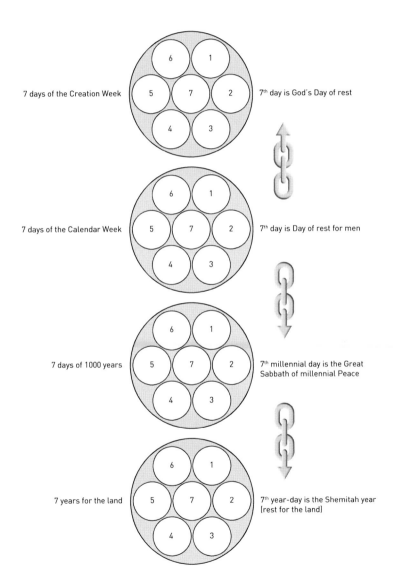

7 days of the Creation Week — 7th day is God's Day of rest

7 days of the Calendar Week — 7th day is Day of rest for men

7 days of 1000 years — 7th millennial day is the Great Sabbath of millennial Peace

7 years for the land — 7th year-day is the Shemitah year (rest for the land)

When we dig there are hidden treasures in God's Word that will be revealed to prune our discipleship and priorities in life.[1]

---

1  Dan. 12:4.

# Chapter Four

# THE CHURCH OR ISRAEL

## —AN EARTHLY BATTLE?

**Church History and the Jews**

This chapter may be upsetting – so please fasten your seat belts! Despite the prophecy that the last days would attract many false teachers[1], please remember while reading that we want to remain thankful for the insights of many Church fathers and the restoration of Biblical truth in the Reformation.

There is much confusion today about the Church and Israel. Some feel it is not important or too divisive to discuss; some follow Replacement Theology that believes that the Church has become the spiritual Israel of God; some believe that the Church and Israel have a totally different role in the end times (strict Dispensationalism); some believe that neither the people nor the land of Israel have any God given calling today. However, we believe that there will finally be unity in the last days between the "Israel of God" and the "Gentiles of God", all being circumcised of heart.[2]

In the first four centuries there was a growing separation between the Church and its Hebraic roots. On the one side it is true that the freedom in Christ did battle with circumcision in the flesh, so that Paul had to rebuke Peter for not eating with gentiles.[3] On the other side, we see many other influences that wrongly caused a further division, especially influenced by Greek philosophers like Plato. These Greek thinkers declared that the material world was evil which led to self-flagellation and asceticism; Greek mythology led to the veneration of saints and icons; Emperor Constantine wrote a Confession of Faith renouncing the feasts of the Hebrews; early Church leaders such as Eusebius, John Chrysostom and Augustine spoke against 'the Jews because they "had killed Christ". They did not see God's Plan behind the crucifixion and His resurrection. Unfortunately these writings and events and man-made theologies were the roots of centuries of anti-Semitism.

---

1   Matt. 24:24.
2   Eph. 2:11-16.
3   Gal. 2:11-14.

Sadly, as very few could read the (Latin) Scriptures in those days, people had to believe what they were told. The Church forgot that Paul wished he might be banished from Christ if this would mean salvation for his Jewish brothers.[1] But these early Church leaders no longer felt the need to be associated with a scattered people and a desolate land, forgetting that they had been grafted into the True Olive. The call of Paul to make the Jews jealous for the Gospel had been cancelled by Replacement Theology.[2] The Church became part of the powerhouse of the Roman empire and Christianity became State religion. It was, indeed, the spiritual Dark Ages of Christianity.

In the middle ages Jewish believers had to make a public confession rejecting their Jewish descent and ancestry before they could be baptised. Christians kidnapped Jewish children as an act of love to baptize them as Christians 'to escape hell fire'! In 1215 the Fourth Lateran Council decreed that Jews must wear a mark to prevent a relationship between Jewish men and Christian women. In 1492 the Inquisition helped drive the Jews from European countries. Hitler only continued a long established practice of marking the Jews as outcasts.

Then came Luther and the Reformation. At first he wrote against Jewish persecution and wrote a thesis 'That Jesus was born as a Jew'. How refreshing! Later, when no Jews had turned to Christ voluntarily, he wrote an essay about, 'The Jews and their lies' in the most terrible language, with a seven point plan of persecution to deal with 'the Jewish Problem.' During Crystal Night in 1938 the Nazis killed Jews and burnt synagogues, just as Luther had recommended.

While Greek culture had encouraged asceticism and a division of body and soul, Roman culture encouraged legalism and bureaucracy. This also influenced the image of God that some churches preached. But the Jews saw that God, a fatherly teacher, had given the Torah as *an instruction for life*. The Hebrew approach is to see no separation between body

---

1  Rom. 9:1-5.
2  Rom. 11:11.

and soul and spirit so that we can worship God with our whole heart, soul and mind. The Greeks put man in the centre, the Jews place God in the centre. The Greeks believe our image of God comes through mental analysis, the Jews believe we can only know God by obedient faith and the study of His Word. The Greeks want to know about God, the Jews want to know Him.

For many centuries the Bible was not available to the laity, while Jewish children were encouraged from an early age to study and meditate on the Tanakh (our Old Testament). Constantine insisted that Christians met in a Church, but Rabbis declared that the home was also a sanctuary and house of prayer. Within Judaism the mutual study of God's Word is the highest form of worship, preparing the way for House Churches today. Christians thought the Jews were seduced by food and drink at their feasts, when in fact the Jews saw the table and food as an altar, and celebrated as God had commanded them.

But God moved to fulfil His plan for His people. From the 17$^{th}$ century Scottish Presbyterians and English Puritans received the vision of the Jews returning to the Promised Land as a result of studying the Word of God. The Old Testament was once again brought back with the New Testament as the undivided Word of God.

Sir Isaac Newton in 1733 and later the Christian leaders of the United States were proponents of the restoration of the State of Israel. The replacement belief that the restoration of Israel in Zechariah 12 had been fulfilled in Christ and His body, the Church, was starting to be rejected. Eventually the unconditional right of the Jews to return to their land was recognised by the Balfour Declaration in 1917.

Then came the satanic counter-attack. Hitler praised Martin Luther in 1923 and believed he was led by God to drive out the Jews, as Jesus had driven out the moneylenders from the temple. He was supported by theologian Gerhard Kittel and felt encouraged by the teachings of a number of early Church fathers. So the spirit of the age led even many

THE CHURCH OR ISRAEL — AN EARTHLY BATTLE?

leaders in the Church to condone the extermination of Jews in Concentration Camps.

Since then there has been some repentance. In 1984 the Evangelical Lutheran Church in America admitted the connection between the heritage of Luther and the Holocaust. The Roman Catholic Church have now retreated from their former anti-Jewish attitude. However, Pope Francis said in 2016 that all religions lead to the same God – a view shared by many post-modern Christian groups!

Fortunately, many Christians believe that Jews and Gentiles can equally receive deliverance and redemption through personal faith in Messiah Yeshua. As the apostle Paul wrote, *'For there is no difference between the Jew or the Greek. For the same Lord over all is generous to all who call upon Him.'* [1]

What will happen to the historic Church to the extent that it persecuted or supported the persecution of the broken off Hebrew branches and even the messianic Jewish ones that were still connected to this Tree? What will happen to many current churches who seem to exist outside the True Olive Tree. Will their blindness lead them into the End Time apostate Church led by the false prophet? We can only pray that all churches will be delivered by the Truth.

In the last days there will be a tsunami of hatred against Israel. *'Come, let us wipe them out as a nation, let the name of Israel be remembered no more.'*[2] Worldwide chaos will follow, millions will die and leaders will hide in caves from the wrath of the Lamb.[3] The believing Jews will be protected by God. They will realise they have been deceived and will turn to accept Jesus as their Messiah. Then Jesus will come, as He left, on the Mount of Olives. The satanic armies will be destroyed by Jesus.[4]

---

1  Rom. 10:12.
2  Ps. 83:4.
3  Rev. 6:15-17.
4  Joel 3:2 & Rev.19:11-16.

All this is a solemn reminder that Christianity was originally Hebrew and that its first leaders were Jewish. But the early Church distanced itself from the True Olive Tree, being deceived by the lie that the Jews deserved their fate because they had murdered Jesus. So the Church came under the influence of Greece, Rome and other pagan sources and lost its true identity as 'one new man in Christ.' Instead many Christians have often seen themselves as the new spiritual Israel, replacing God's Covenant people. They are divided into many factions. Some of their writings inspired the worst genocide in history.

This is in no way to denigrate great examples of people of faith in Church history, nor to deny the truth revealed in many theological writings. But now is the time for the Bride to prepare herself to meet the Bridegroom and be guided by the Word and not man made religious teaching. Now is the time for messianic Jews and Gentiles to recognise that they are together the one new man – the Bride of Christ.

Then they will rejoice together in the next most beautiful chapter of God-given feasts with all their significance for discipleship and the beauty of the Bride.

# Chapter Five

# GOD'S PLAN HIDDEN IN SEVEN FEASTS

## AND THEIR
## NEW COVENANT MEANING

## Introduction

God instructed Moses to celebrate special feasts, but the Church today rarely does so, because it is believed the feasts were for the Jews. But we will discover that all feasts have in Jesus Christ a deep New Covenant meaning and deserve a place in Christian practice. As Jesus fulfilled the four Spring feasts during His first coming, will He not also fulfil the last three Autumn feasts on His return?

## God Uses Another Calendar

God told Moses to move the start of the original calendar year 6 months earlier from the 7th autumn month Tishri back to make the spring month, Nisan, the first month of the year.[1] In this way the spring and autumn feasts would reflect God's plan of salvation for mankind in the right order. However, as the Hebrew calendar is based on lunar and solar cycles, Israel has added an extra month every two or three years to keep the feasts at the appropriate time in their season.

Today most calendars are based on the Gregorian calendar but this can hide important dates on the Hebrew calendar. For instance, the 9th day of the Hebrew month of Av is when Jews read the book of Lamentations. On this day ten of the twelve spies to the promised land brought back a bad report; the first and second temples were destroyed on this day; the first world war started and in 1942 Hitler started deporting Jews to extermination camps – all on this calendar day. These are just a few examples.

## The Feasts are His feasts, to be celebrated on the appointed times

God appointed the feasts of the Lord not just for the Jews but also for the Gentiles who would follow into God's rest. The holy convocations were called 'mikrah Kodesh' which also means 'holy rehearsals.'[2] It is not often realised that the giving of the Torah on Mount Sinai is the same calendar date as the giving of the Holy Spirit 50 days after Passover at Pentecost. The feasts were meant to remember and look back at great moments in

---

1 Ex. 12:2.
2 Lev. 23:2.

covenant with God, but also to look forward to what God has promised in the future. The feasts lead up to the 'barley', 'wheat' and 'grape' harvests of souls and should mirror the spiritual walk of the believer.

## Validity of the Feasts

The church, remembering that Jesus talked of 'another stable', assumed that these feasts were not for them.[1] How can this be? Jesus celebrated the feasts[2], Paul taught that the New Covenant meaning of the feasts had to become part of their walk of faith.[3] He was also anxious to be back in Jerusalem for Pentecost, as he wanted to continue celebrate God's appointed times, in a new covenant way, and he wanted to reach out to his own people as well.[4]

The Feasts are important to God. Zechariah foretold that in the Millennium of Peace the fulfilled Feast of Tabernacles would still be celebrated and that nations who refuse would get no rain![5] God told Moses that these feasts were appointed as an everlasting statute throughout all generations.[6] These feasts simply belong to the stem of the Olive Tree, of which Christ is the root, and point to our future with Him. They were practised by the very early church, but were finally forbidden because of increasing enmity between the Church and Jews.

## A Misunderstanding about Feasts

'These religious practices are **only** a shadow of what was coming – the body that cast the shadow is Christ'. Colossians 2:16-17.

This suggests that the feasts reflected Christ and were therefore abolished at His coming. But the word '**only**' is not in the original text, and has been taken out in the New King James version. The feasts are in fact a shadow of Jesus Christ who has come and who is to come again. So

---

1   John 10:16.
2   Mark 14:12.
3   1 Cor. 5: 8.
4   Acts 20:16, 1 Cor. 9:20.
5   Zech. 14:17.
6   Lev. 23:14.

Paul instructs gentile believers to stay away from their former pagan feasts but to celebrate God's feasts in their New Covenant way. Very sadly, Emperor Constantine mixed pagan feasts with biblical feasts and thereafter sowed confusion in the Church. Only today do we begin to understand that the New Testament should be read as the Old Testament revealed.

### Shadows are the test of the spiritual perception of postmodernists

The postmodern mind-set creates truth to suit the individual; God is too big to be understood so one person can only see some of the many facets of God; the idea is that we should not impose our theological views on others; postmodernists claim that with other religions we all believe in the same God and the Bible has to be interpreted in a way that is acceptable to modern society. We disagree: only when we demonstrate a walk of faith that corresponds to the reality in Christ of all the feasts will we show that we are in Christ Who is the only Truth and will we be able to better discern the false concepts of contemporary society.

### Why does our perception deviate from reality?

Our perception of Jesus Christ is subjective. Pictures of Mary and Jesus painted in different countries often do not describe the reality of a Jewish woman of those days. Few believers fully realise that our understanding of Christ is affected by our culture, our education, our circumstances and even our willingness to study and dig for the truth.

### Humanism Has Also Influenced Theological Thinking

Man was made in the image of God, but nowadays man wants to make God after his own beliefs. Many churches will increasingly have to wrestle with this process of man creating a God Who will conform with an increasingly decadent world. Let us not forget that Paul told us to 'prove all things and hold fast to that which is good.'[7]

The only way to unlearn and learn again is to ask questions. As an example, we have to unlearn the idea that Isaac was a small boy when God told

---

7  1 Thess. 5:21.

Abraham to sacrifice him, as most of the pictures want us to believe. Then learn that Sarah died shortly afterwards, so we can calculate that Isaac was already in his early thirties. He was a type of Jesus Christ, carrying the wood like Jesus, to be sacrificed at the same spot on Mount Moriah where Jesus would be crucified and, just as the first Passover in Egypt, all happening on the 14th day of the month Nisan. With the help of His Word and His Spirit we will confound our adversary who wishes to remove the Old Testament as an anchor of the truth of our beliefs.

**Another reason that the shadow of the Old Testament is important**
The King James Bible was based on the manuscripts of the early Church. Later new manuscripts were used from the School of Alexandria to form modern translations like the Revised Standard Version (RSV). But the Alexandrian School taught Bible texts should be taken more symbolically than literally and even had doubts about the divinity of Christ! The only safe course we can take is to not just rely on existing theologies and modern translations, but to constantly refer back to the early Scriptures which reveal the true shadow pictures.

**More lessons from the shadow of the Old Testament**
Jesus recognised the Old Testament as the source of truth about Himself. On the road to Emmaus He told the two disciples all that the prophets had foretold and what was written about Him in the Scriptures.

**Theologians need other Specialists**
Sir Isaac Newton discovered the Law of Gravity that God had created, but also wrote more books about the Bible and the End Times than about physics. His example shows that theologians need to have the humility to embrace a multi-disciplinary approach and co-operate with God-fearing mathematicians, biologists, physicists, futurists etc. It was this approach that led Sir Donald Anderson to use his police training to unlock a prophecy of Daniel.

## The Biblical Feasts are Christian Feasts

From the Council of Nicea in 325 AD the Church, in its pride, cancelled the biblical feasts. They rejected their Hebrew *'root and branches'* even though Paul had warned them, *'But if some of the branches were broken off.....do not be arrogant towards them...Do not be conceited but fear'.* [1]

It is not being suggested that readers should commemorate the feasts as the Jews have done, nor to go back to the Law of Moses. But rather to celebrate them every day for their specific and very deep relevance to discipleship and **for their prophetic meaning in the New Covenant, because Christ is central to these feasts**.

---

1  Rom. 11:17-29.

## Seven Feasts

There are seven thousand years of history; seven days of creation; seven weeks between first fruits and Pentecost; seven months between the first and last feast; seven years of Tribulation; a Jubilee year after seven times seven years; a 'time' of 7x70 years; seven golden candlesticks as a picture of seven churches; seven stars representing the angels of the seven churches; seven spirits of God; seven seals; seven trumpets; seven bowls of wrath; seven arms of the menorah (the Hebrew candlestick); and seven feasts of God.

The feasts are in three groups:

**Pesach – the Passover**

**Unleavened Bread - Ha' Matzoth**

**Feast of the First Fruits – Ha'Bikkurim**

After 49 days comes:

**Pentecost – Shavuot**. Then after a long hot, dry summer up to the Fall feasts:

**Trumpets – Yom Teruah**

**Atonement – Yom Kippur**

**Tabernacles – Sukkoth**

The 'early rain' falls from October to December to soften the ground and allow crops to be planted. The 'latter rain' falls from March to April to ripen the barley at Pesach and the wheat at Pentecost. We repeat that at the Exodus God changed the start of the religious year from the Fall to the Spring, so that all appointed feasts would fit in their harvest season.

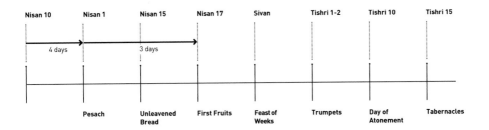

## Pesach – the Passover Festival of Deliverance

At that time the Jews did not see that Passover was a prophetic shadow of the Crucifixion. Yet they were expecting Messiah to come 4 days (4000 years) after Adam and Eve. However, they expected a conqueror to liberate them from Rome, but, except a remnant, God *'blinded their eyes and hardened their hearts'* because of their disobedience.[1] Yet many rulers believed in Him, but secretly, so as not to be thrown out of the Synagogue. [2]

Jacob prophesied that the ruler's staff and sceptre would not depart from Judah until Shiloh (Jesus) would come.[3] When the right of the Sanhedrin to pronounce a death sentence was removed by Rome, 22 years before the crucifixion, they knew that the sceptre had been taken away from them. Because of this fact (and many other biblical facts) they should have seen and recognised the Messiah in their midst. No wonder Stephen berated them for being, *'stiff-necked and uncircumcised in heart and ears'*. [4]

Four days before Pesach, on Nisan 10, the High Priest went to Bethany or Bethlehem to select a perfect lamb for the Temple Pesach offering. There would be a huge crowd around Jerusalem when, according to the historian Josephus, about 275,000 lambs would be selected. Each lamb was kept in a family for four days to be sure it was unblemished. It was no coincidence that, while visiting Lazarus, Jesus's feet were anointed by Mary with oil of spikenard on Nisan 10 to anoint Him for what lay ahead. After all, He would become the Pesach Lamb for the world.

---

1  John 12:40.
2  John 12:42.
3  Gen. 49:10.
4  Acts 7:51.

### The Entrance of the Lamb - Nisan 10

The crowds, because of the raising of Lazarus, treated Jesus as the Messiah, waving palm branches and laying their garments on the road before Him. In acting this way they symbolically lay their dignity before Him, as garments reflected the wealth and status of their owners. They sang, 'Hosanna, blessed is He who comes in the name of the Lord.'[1] Jesus also fulfilled the prophecy that the coming King would ride on a donkey.[2] Yet many of the leaders were blinded. The Talmud still expects the coming Messiah to ride on a donkey, but He already did!

During the next four days, the time of the inspection of the lambs, the Pharisees and Sadducees continually questioned Jesus. They tried to find fault in Jesus to pronounce Him as imperfect. They failed! Even Pilate said He was without sin. Jesus, the Passover Lamb, was examined for four days and found unblemished. These four days also represent the 4000 years waiting for Jesus Christ, and the two days in the tomb reflect the 2000 hidden years before His return.

### The Binding of the Lamb on the Altar

At sunrise of Nisan 14 Jesus carried His Cross, as Isaac carried the firewood. At the third hour, around 9am, the Pesach lamb was bound to the horns of the altar at the same time that Jesus was nailed to the Cross. From the Cross Jesus could probably see the Temple and hear the singing of the Passover service. But as the lambs were slaughtered, darkness covered Jerusalem from around 12 noon until 3pm.

### The Lamb Sacrificed for the Nation

The lamb had to be slaughtered 'between the evenings'. 'The first evening' in Jewish tradition starts at 12 noon and the 'second evening' at the setting of the sun. 'Between the evenings' is about 3pm. So as the Pesach lamb was slaughtered, Jesus may have heard the Levites singing, 'The sorrows of death encompassed me, and the pains of hell got hold of me: I felt trouble and sorrow.'[3]

1  Ps. 118:26.
2  Zech. 9:9.
3  Ps. 116:3.

Jesus laid down His life[4], having born the physical suffering and the spiritual weight of sin. Our Passover lamb died that we might be righteous.

### The Blood of the Pesach Lambs

The blood of about 275,000 lambs, mixed with water, flowed from the altar in the Temple via aqueducts into the Hinnom valley, translated in Greek as 'Gehenna' or 'Hell'. This valley had a horrible history as it had been used for pagan worship and the sacrifice of children to the god Moloch.[5] Was this a shadow picture? When the Lamb of God shed His blood and water from the Cross, He then went down to visit the generation of Noah in prison. [6]

A shadow of Calvary had already been seen by the Jews when the blood of the first Passover Lambs was placed on the top and both sides of the door posts of their houses in Egypt. Jesus said He was the door, and that all who enter, as in Egypt, would be safe.[7]

In ancient Hebrew we can discover an amazing sign for the phrase, 'Alpha and Omega', the First and the Last. The picture sign of 'Alpha' (Aleph) is the head of a horned ox, the leader of the herd, the strongest, the first. The picture of 'and' (Vav) is a nail. The ancient Hebrew picture of Omega (Tav) is a cross. As we can see below, in ancient Hebrew this pictured that Jesus was the **Leader nailed on a Cross.**

| Old Semitic | Meaning | Modern Hebrew | English |
|---|---|---|---|
| ƴ | The leader, the first, the strongest | א | Aleph |
| Y | The nail, the pin | ı | Vav |
| † | The cross, two crossed sticks | ת | Tav |

---

4  John 10:18.
5  2 King 23:10.
6  1 Peter 3:18-20.
7  John 10:9.

## Good Friday?

We know that Jesus rode into Jerusalem on Palm Sunday as it was Nisan 10, followed by four days for the 'inspection of the lamb'. On our Wednesday evening, the start of Nisan 14, Jesus was arrested and crucified on Thursday, still Nisan 14, before the High Sabbath of the first day of Unleavened Bread that was on the Friday that year. Then followed the three nights of the Sign of Jonah before the resurrection on Sunday morning that was also the day of the third Feast, the Feast of First Fruits. **The Christian misunderstanding about Good Friday has been caused by their rejection of their Jewish roots!** But Jesus fulfilled every Spring feast on the exact calendar day.

## King of the Jews

Pilate put 'The King of the Jews' on the Cross in Latin, usually abbreviated as INRI. But it was also written in Greek and Hebrew. The Hebrew reads:

**Y**eshua **H**anotzri **V**emelech **H**ayehudim – or "YHVH" – which is the abbreviated name of God. Is this coincidence? The Jews did put their family name on the neck of their lamb; God put His name on His Passover Lamb on the Cross.

## No Bone shall be Broken

The Jewish leaders asked Pilate to have the bones of the three crucified men broken so as to expedite their death by asphyxiation. This was because the next day (Friday) was the High Sabbath and the start of the Feast of Unleavened Bread, followed by the weekly Sabbath on the Saturday and by the Feast of the First Fruits on the following Sunday.

But 1500 years earlier the Most High had commanded that no bone of the Pesach lamb was to be broken. The Jews at that time had no idea why, but it foreshadowed what was yet to come at the time of Jesus crucifixion. Jesus **laid down His life** after being on the Cross for only six hours, compared to some who died after two days on the Cross. Once again Jesus fulfilled the shadow, as in the Temple the Lamb of the Nation was also tied to the horns of the altar for six hours. What a wonder that Jesus fulfilled Pesach so completely!

## His Clothes were not Torn

Priests had a robe without a seam, so did Jesus. His robe was not torn, but gambled for, seemingly to fulfil a prophecy.[1] God had said to Moses that the robe of Aaron, the high priest was not to be torn.[2]

When Jesus did not deny that He was the Messiah, the High Priest Caiaphas disobeyed the Law when he tore his clothes and so was removed from the High Priesthood by God. Earlier, Jesus had been baptized by John, not into a baptism of repentance, but the ritually required baptism into the Priesthood.[3] Jesus was the substitute Sacrificial Lamb, as John had announced,[4] but after His atoning sacrifice, He also became the new High Priest after the order of Melchizedek.[5]

## The Veil of the Temple was Torn

This was not just to indicate access to the Father through the blood of Jesus. When Jacob heard that Joseph had seemingly died, he tore his mantle from top to bottom as a sign of deep grief over the death of his son. The veil in the Temple was, as it were, God's mantle, torn with grief over His Son. Soon the earthly Temple would be destroyed, but we still have a Temple in heaven where Jesus is our High Priest and Advocate between our Father and us.

## Jews do believe in the Suffering Messiah

Many Jews do believe that Yeshua was a great man, even a prophet, but find it hard to accept the idea of a man dying for another. They believe that **Isaiah 53** refers to Israel and not to Messiah, although rabbinic writings in the pre-Christian Talmud do speak of a Messiah suffering for the sins of others. '*When God desires healing to the world, He smites one*

---

1 Ps. 22:19.
2 Lev. 10:6.
3 Ex. 29:4.
4 John 1:29.
5 Ps.110:4 & Hebr. 5:6.

*righteous man among them with suffering and through him gives healing to all.'* [1] Let us biblically test and then use these Jewish sources to reach out to non-messianic Jews!

## New Testament Meaning of Pesach

The 'Passover' of death and liberation from slavery was just the beginning for the Jews. It was the start, as it is for a Christian, of their life of faith, fighting their desire to return to the 'fleshpots of Egypt' by staying in obedience to God.

A Jewish Midrash suggests that many Jews died of unbelief in the plague of darkness[2]. Most also stayed in the comfort of Babylon rather than face the rigours of a return to Jerusalem. It is the same for nominal Christians who one day will hear Jesus say, *'Be gone, I never knew you.'* [3]

## The Golden Calf

Less than two months after leaving Egypt, the Jews were alone in the desert without a leader[4]. Moses had disappeared up Mount Sinai and they did not know if he would return. They had been living for four hundred years in the pagan climate of Egypt. Under this influence they went back to the Egyptian god they knew, probably Apis, a calf with a golden sun between his horns. Later king Jeroboam restored the worship of the golden calf in Israel to prevent people going up to Jerusalem. Let us be careful not to return to slavery!

## Nisan 14  The Passover on God's Calendar

You can see a particular pattern emerging on God's Calendar, but it's only visible on the Hebrew Calendar. Jesus made clear that He was the reality of the Old Testament shadow on Nisan 14, when he was crucified as the Pesach Lamb for the World. It was the same calendar date on which Isaac was bound on the altar and the Pesach lamb was slaughtered in Egypt. The Pesach ritual was repeated every year in the Temple,

---

1  Zohar 5:218a.
2  Rashi about Ex. 10:22, Mechilta, Tanchuma, Beshallach 1.
3  Matth. 7:23.
4  Ex. 32:1-6.

but the Jews did not recognise its fulfilment when Jesus laid down His life on **Nisan 14.** As always, there was God's perfect coincidence of the shadow with the reality.

## Nisan 15 - The Feast of Unleavened Bread

Jesus died without sin at the end of the day of the 14th day of Nisan. The Feast of Unleavened Bread, lasting 7 days, started on the 15th day of Nisan. On that calendar date the Hebrew slaves had to flee Egypt hastily. Because of that they ate bread without yeast. The tradition of removing yeast from your house is based on a biblical commandment.[5]

It is still tradition that Jewish houses go through a great cleansing before the start of the Spring Feasts. This shadow is the outer expression of the need for an inner search for sins hidden in our hearts – our spiritual house. *'Purge out the old leaven, that you may be a new lump, as you are unleavened...let us keep the feast with the unleavened bread of sincerity and truth'.* [6]

Jews who were eating leavened bread during this Feast were removed from the community. This is a picture of those who want to hold on to their sin and so cannot remain with God's people. Topics like sin, punishment and judgement are seldom taught today because, *'God is love and we live in a time of grace.'* But if we are serious about our Covenant with God, we will always be removing the leaven from our lives, just as a bride prepares herself for her bridegroom.

## Nisan 15 – Jesus in the Grave

As we have already seen God is doing special things on special calendar dates to show us the patterns in His plan of Salvation. There is also a fascinating picture around Nisan 15: Jesus was in Hades on Nisan 15 visiting the spirits in prison who were disobedient from the days of Noah.[7] He had the keys of Death and Hades who had no power over Him. This was also the calendar day that the Egyptians buried their firstborn;

5   Ex. 12:15.
6   1 Cor. 5:7-8.
7   1 Peter 3:19.

according to Jewish tradition this was also the day that the sinful cities of Sodom and Gomorrah were destroyed as well as the day that Daniel was in the Lion's den. It is the story of judgement and deliverance!

On this day the Jews left Egypt and Lot left Sodom hastily. They had to leave their possessions behind. Lot's wife looked back and turned into a pillar of salt as a terrible warning not to hang on to the world with all its attractions. When the Son of man comes, those on the roof and those in the field are not to look back to get their possessions. We are all called to remember the unleavened bread, which means to remove sin and to place God above everything else in our lives. Jesus said, 'Those who love me will obey me!'[1]

**Feast of First Fruits - Ha'Bikkurim**
The third Spring Feast starts on the day after the first Sabbath after the High Sabbath of Pesach, which, in that year of His death was on Nisan 17, the third day after the crucifixion. The barley had been sown in the winter of the year before and was now ripe for harvest. To obey the Law, priests went out to cut the first ripe barley after sunset to be waved before God in the Temple at the beginning of the feast. Jesus also rose from death to life at this time, presenting Himself as a wave offering to God as, 'the first fruits of those who have died.'[2]

By bringing in the first barley harvest, waved by the High Priest before God, the people showed that they trusted God for His further blessing on the harvests that would follow. At this harvest time farmers made an often long journey to Jerusalem with their first fruits before they harvested the rest. When Mary met Jesus in the garden He had not yet ascended to the Father as a wave offering of the first fruit. That was the true reason that He asked Mary not to touch Him.[3] Then He returned for forty days to earth, followed by His Ascension.[4]

1 John 14:23.
2 1 Cor. 15:20.
3 John 20:17.
4 Acts 1:9.

The grain of barley is the picture of someone who follows Jesus with all his heart. Middle East barley has a soft casing that is lightly roasted and then separated from the grain by the wind (a picture of the Holy Spirit) when it is thrown into the air. Does it surprise us that Christians are tested by fire through many tribulations before they are harvested in the air at the Rapture? Moreover, at harvest the barley plant is pulled up completely, leaving nothing behind!

The parallel between Pesach and the crucifixion continues. Some days before the Feast of the First Fruits, messengers from the Sanhedrin went out to the field where barley grew for the Temple. They tied the chosen sheaves together with a ribbon but the stalks were not cut off yet. Is this not a picture of Jesus being tied by messengers from the Sanhedrin on the same evening before His crucifixion?

There is another parallel. The Jews were slaves of Pharaoh, and by Egyptian law their slavery could only end on the date of death of their owner. The Jews left Egypt on the 15th of Nisan, and Pharaoh was drowned on the 17th of Nisan, setting the captives free as the first fruits on the calendar date of that feast.

**Baptism as a Sign of Conversion**
There is a strong connection between baptism as a sign of conversion and the journey through the Red Sea and it fits in the order of the God given feasts.

The Jews used baptism in ritual baths (mikveh) for cleansing and also when a gentile wanted to convert to Judaism.

Infant baptism in traditional churches can be a beautiful and honest sign to God. Even though the child is already sanctified, if it has believing parents, it is given back to God with a prayer for help to nurture the child in the knowledge of God. But this is not the believer's baptism required by God, since baptism is the answer of a good conscience toward God.[1]

Baptism reflects dying from the bondage of sin (Egypt) and rising to new life at the other side of the Red Sea.

Baptism also reflects the experience of the Hebrew Slaves who went through the Red Sea, after being liberated from the bondage of slavery. What do you think the slaves thought when they stood before the Red Sea? They thought they were going to die! In baptism it is the same. Believers confess they are going to die, to lay down their lives and to die with Christ, so that they will rise with Him in newness of life. As Paul said, 'I die daily.'[2] But he also said that we would join the resurrected Jesus in the new life, referring to the First Fruits following the sacrifice of Pesach.[3]

## What is the Purpose of Deliverance?

We have not been liberated so that God can bless us with success and material blessing. We have been set free to serve God, and if we don't serve Him, it is likely that we will fall back into our old ways. Instead we will have, like the Jews in their 40-year wandering in the wilderness, a time of testing to bring us to spiritual maturity. We must resist falling away just because we don't feel His presence personally in our life; when prayers are not answered in the way we want; when we feel bewildered, like Job. Yet with all the trials, we have the Instructions of His Word and the guidance of the Holy Spirit. Provided we are dressed in His armour, He helps us to be overcomers in all circumstances.

## Another Future Exodus

God called Moses to break the bonds of Pharaoh and in the whole Exodus story we see he is a shadow of Jesus Christ who broke the bonds of satan. His blood applied to the Cross of Calvary was the starting point

---

1   1 Pet. 3:21.
2   1 Cor. 15:31.
3   Rom. 6:4-5.

of a much larger Exodus under the blood of the Pesach Lamb of God. But there is still a future exodus to come when all of remaining mankind will eventually be freed from the hands of the authorities and the powers in heavenly places, after which the new heaven and earth will be a fact. Once again we will see that the Pharaoh of this world, the antichrist, will do all he can to prevent this Exodus. Revelation shows us that there will be a great battle. But after many judgements, the returning King of kings will usher in the Millennium of Peace. Finally the New Heaven and Earth will appear.

**The Seventeenth Day of Nisan**
God did remarkable things on remarkable calendar days;

On this 17th day:

- the Ark of Noah landed on Mount Ararat: a new beginning for the **earth.**

- the Israelites are on the far side of the Red Sea: a new beginning for a **people.**

- the Israelites ate the first fruits of the land: the annual rebirth of **agriculture**.

- the defeat of Satan: Christ was resurrected. The rebirth of the **one new man in Christ made possible**.

This perfect alignment of dates shows God's complete control of history and time.

We also recognise the weekly Sabbath as a rehearsal of the rest that is to come, the Great Sabbath of the Millennium of Peace. Jesus said that the Sabbath was meant to be a blessing to us, when we could put aside what we normally do and be reminded of the rest He calls us to.[4] We are called

4  Matt. 11.29.

51

not to miss His rest by disobedience, but to cease from our labours and strive to enter our rest in Christ.[1]

### The Feast of Weeks – Pentecost – Shavuot

The Feast of Weeks is on the fiftieth ('Penta' = 50) day after the Feast of First Fruit. The first Feast of Weeks was at Mount Sinai, 50 days after the Jews left Egypt, when God confirmed His Covenant with them. At Pentecost, after Jesus' ascension, God gave His New Covenant to the Jews, by pouring out His Spirit. Later Gentiles, who believed in Yeshua, were added to the Body of Christ. On this day, a wave offering of two loaves in the morning represented the Jews and the Gentiles united in Christ.

### The Attack of the Amalekites

Cleansing and deliverance by the blood of Jesus does not guarantee peaceful circumstances. Let's look at the shadow picture. Before the freed Hebrew slaves came to Mount Sinai, where God would confirm the Covenant with this people, Amalek, the sons of Esau, fought to destroy the Jews at Rephidim.[2] This is how the adversary operates. It was because of the prayers of Moses and the strength of Joshua (a picture of Christ) that these Amalekites were defeated. This is also why especially new believers need prayers for God's protection.

### Freedom and Commandments

The Jews had been redeemed from the slavery of Egypt and its gods but they needed Moses and the Torah to give them a new understanding of how to live in obedience to God. Freedom means nothing unless it has a purpose and a power to take responsibility for one's actions. At Sinai God's finger wrote the Ten Commandments, on which the Jews meditated. At Pentecost, after Jesus' ascension, the Holy Spirit started to engrave the law of Christ in the hearts of those belonging to the Body of Christ. He also gave believers spiritual gifts and boldness to enable them to walk as Jesus walked.[3]

---

1  Hebr. 4:11.
2  Ex. 17:8-13.
3  Eph. 6, 1 John 2:6.

### Does the Holy Spirit make the Law Obsolete?

The Midrash, the rabbinical comments on Bible verses, has Rabbi Johanan saying that when God gave the Torah on Mount Sinai there were individual flames on each person. Also, the Voice of God was heard in seventy languages to show that the Torah was for all nations.[4] So when the disciples spoke in foreign tongues at Pentecost they knew from the calendar date and from these comments that God was connecting this New Testament Pentecost to the old Pentecost (or Feast of Weeks).

Since we have become the Body of Christ in word and deed, the Holy Spirit has **intensified** the Word and wants to intensify our spiritual life so that our righteousness exceeds that of the Pharisees, while we fulfil the law of Christ.[5] He has also **internalised** the Word that is now engraved on our hearts as we study His Word, guided by the Holy Spirit. It has also **internationalised** the Word that is now available to the co-heirs, the believers in all nations. All this enables us to obey the Law of Christ through Spirit rather than just the letter of the Law, so that we can make progress in loving God and our neighbour better than before.

### Is the Law Really Reduced to Two Commandments?

The Law has been misunderstood and reduced by many Christians as something that determines an offence and as the basis for penalty. Christians do believe we are not saved by keeping the law. We are saved by grace through faith that the blood of Jesus has washed us clean. The Jews, however, saw the Torah as an instruction, a 'constitution of freedom', to help them live in the freedom God has given. Sadly, Christians often want to be liberated from the Law, when in fact the Spirit uses the whole Word to guide them every moment how to love God and their neighbour from their heart, and in doing so to fulfil the Law of Christ.

### An Important Difference in Harvesting

The barley at the Feast of First Fruits was tossed in the wind to separate the chaff from the grain. Jesus was the First Fruit of the barley harvest.

---

4  Shemot Midrash Rabbah 5:9.
5  Gal. 6:2.

Then at Pentecost comes the wheat harvest. Wheat has to be crushed to release the grains. Some see this as a symbol of those who repent during the Great Tribulation and also of the Foolish Virgins who have to be 'crushed' in the tribulation to enter the Kingdom. Let us pray that as many Jews and Gentiles as possible will be in the barley harvest.

### The New Feast of Pentecost – God's Glory Returns

Just before the Babylonian exile, God's Presence left the temple in Jerusalem.[1] At Pentecost the priest used to bring the wave offering of two leavened loaves, representing Jews & Gentiles, at 9am – the third hour. At the same moment, to show that God was following the pattern of His feasts, the presence of God returned as the fire of the Holy Spirit on the disciples, now themselves temples of God and a Royal Priesthood.[2]

However, we still need to **choose** to follow His Word with all of our heart, mind and strength with the assistance of the Holy Spirit. Man is still free to choose, but is never free from the consequences of his choice. At the first Pentecost at Mount Sinai God came to live among His people. They went away from Him and later suffered the 70 year exile as one of the consequences of not taking His Instructions seriously. But at the Pentecost, after Jesus' ascension, God's Glory returned and, as Paul says, we must now obey the call to sanctify our lives very seriously.[3]

### How do we celebrate the Spring Feasts?

Jesus said that He had not come to destroy God's Instructions, which included the celebration of Feasts.[4] When the Church gave up the Feasts, they lost a great stimulation to the quality and depth of discipleship in Christ. At Pentecost God put his Presence in all born-again Christians. They are temple of the Holy Spirit. So Paul writes, '*Know ye not that ye are the Temple of God and that the Spirit of God dwells within you?*'[5] This verse implies that we no longer have to go to a place to follow a ritual. We now

---

1   Ez. 10.
2   Acts 2:15, 1 Pet. 1:1, 2:5.
3   2 Cor. 6:16-18.
4   Matt 5:17.
5   1 Cor. 3:16.

can celebrate the message of the Spring Feasts fulfilled in Christ, daily and ever more deeply at the place where we are.

**What can the Church Learn from the Sequence of the Feasts?**
Christian denominations are divided, partly because they have lost touch with the meaning of the feasts and the reality they portray in Christ. Some Christians do not take communion because they are not sure they are redeemed. They have not seen that all God required was that the Jews should be **obedient** to put the blood on the door posts and then **trust** that death would pass over. That was already redemption by grace through faith. In some denominations the God of the Psalms may be seen by some as a vengeful God, with damnation preached for our sins. This is contrary to the initial mercy of Passover, because Jesus came to save and not to judge.[6] The sequence of the Feasts is therefore so important.

On the other hand, in some churches it is taught that God no longer remembers our (current and future) sins during our discipleship walk because they have already been forgiven on the Cross. Although Paul says we are free of the, *'works of the Law'*, he does not say that the Law has been abolished. Yes, Jesus has delivered us from the power of sin, but we are also called to fight off sins that tempt us. The message of the Feast of Unleavened Bread is to remind us to keep the leaven of sin from our lives.[7]

Liberal Christians find the gift of God's Instruction difficult – they rather want to be free from rules. Instead, they say, they want to follow the Holy Spirit. But freedom from the Law of Christ is a form of rebellion. Real freedom comes from obedience to God, as Jesus said, *'If anyone loves me, he will keep my commandments.'*[8] It is the same in the Old Testament. There God described the blessings that would follow obedience and the curses that would follow disobedience. The decision to obey or disobey is up to each believer.[9]

---

6  John 3:17.
7  Rom. 7:24.
8  John 14:23.
9  Deut. 28.

**Cups of Wine during the Seder (Passover) Meal**

The Seder meal in **Exodus 12** did not include wine, but in the lifetime of Jesus this meal included four cups of wine to remember the Exodus' promises of God:

1. I will **deliver** you from the forced labour of the Egyptians.

2. I will **set you free** from slavery.

3. I will **redeem** you with an outstretched arm.

4. I will **adopt** you to be My people and to be your God.

The order of these cups shows us the pattern of the Spring Feasts. At the first cup people are **delivered** from Egypt, represented by Pesach. At the second cup they are **freed** from Egyptian idols and ideas and from the slavery of sin, represented by the Feast of Unleavened Bread. That they were **redeemed** was remembered on the Feast of First Fruits when Pharaoh, their legal owner, was drowned with his army in the Red Sea. Finally their **adoption as a covenant people** by God is recorded at the Feast of Weeks with the giving of the Law on Mount Sinai.

God also said in Exodus, '*I will* **bring** *you to the Promised Land and I will* **give** *it into your possession.*' In conjunction with this promise, there is a fifth cup that is poured but not drunk. This awaits the coming of Messiah to complete the promises. It is called the cup of Elijah for his second coming. This points to the moment when God gives the Promised Land to His people in the Millennium, to be followed by the New Jerusalem coming down from Heaven.[1]

So, **to summarise**, the Spring Feasts and their significance were as follows:

**Nisan 10** - Jesus, the Lamb of God, enters Jerusalem to be inspected for purity.

---

1  Rev. 21:2.

**Nisan 14 -** Pesach (Passover), cleansing and deliverance from slavery by His blood on the Cross of Calvary.

**Nisan 15 -** Unleavened Bread, Jesus, Who had no sin, entered Hades. We are to be an unleavened bread of sincrety and truth.

**Nisan 17 -** First Fruits, Jesus' resurrection at the calendar day of the crossing of the Red Sea. We are to walk as a new creation in Christ, as a first fruit in Him.

**The month of Sivan:** Feast of Weeks (Pentecost); receiving God's Instruction (The Law of Christ) by the Holy Spirit written on our hearts. Living in covenant with Him.

### The Fall Feasts and their Prophetic Meanings

There is a long dry summer between the Spring feasts and the start of the Autumn feasts. This period is a shadow picture of the long period of Church history from the fulfilment of Pentecost until the return of Christ. Hardly any rain falls, reminiscent of the dark ages of the Church. Maybe the last centuries can be compared to the period of the latter rain, just before the harvest begins. Finally, Daniel's prophecy is now being fulfilled that some matters would remain sealed until the Last Days. The Fall is the time of the fruit harvest of grapes and olives that speak of the produce of our lives in Christ that we will present to the Bridegroom – Jesus Christ.

The three autumn feasts are:

### The Feast of Trumpets (Yom Teru'ah) – Tishri 1

This Feast is also known as Rosh HaShanah, the Head of the Year. It starts on the first calendar day of the 7th month, which is called the month of Tishri. The preceding month of Elul is called the period of Teshuvah (repentance), in which all are called to 40 days of repentance and a decision to return to the right way and to refrain from things that grieve God as we prepare to meet the King. The Feast starts on the first day of the month Tishri when there are ten 'days of Awe' for people to consider their position before God – what about sin in their lives and have they got oil in their lamps? The Feast of Trumpets anticipates the sounding of the last trumpet before Yeshua returns in glory, after the Church of Christ has been gathered up in the Rapture. [1]

**The Day of Atonement** (Yom Kippur) – Tishri 10
This celebrates national forgiveness by God and looks forward to the return of Jesus Christ to the Mount of Olives. Our High Priest will return at the end of the Great Tribulation when His reconciliation with all of Israel will also be fulfilled.

**The Feast of Tabernacles** (Sukkot) – Tishri 15 – 22
This looks forward to the start of the Millennium when Jesus Christ will establish His kingdom on earth and sit on the throne of David in Jerusalem, a time of celebration.

Jesus Christ will fulfil these Feasts Himself. There will be seven years of increasing Global Tribulation between the final Feast of Trumpets and the final Day of Atonement, followed a few days later by the fulfilment of the Feast of Tabernacles when Jesus has returned to usher in the Millennium.

**The Month of Elul – Prepare yourself for the King!**
The month of Elul precedes the festival month of Tishri. The first day of Elul was the time Moses climbed Mount Sinai for the **second** time to plead for the people for forty days after their idolatry with the golden calf. When Moses returned with God's merciful forgiveness on the fortieth day, it was called the Day of Atonement.

Traditionally this "season of repentance" is used:

- to repent and turn back to God

- to be reconciled with those we have hurt

- to care for the needy

---

1   1 Thess. 4:16, 1 Cor.15:52.

This is a good time to look out for any 'golden calves' in our lives that we may 'worship' or give our attention to; to seek out and forgive those who have hurt us; to remember our call to help the poor. When the Rapture comes, there will be no time to buy oil for our lamps. We cannot be passive when we are called to prepare ourselves as the Bride - hence the blowing of the Shofar (ram's horn) to help us to WAKE UP – hence the title of this book!

## The Feast of Trumpets - The Mystery of the Last Trumpet

This Feast, sadly not found in the Christian Calendar, is the most hopeful Feast for believers in the 21st century. It is soon to be fulfilled! The Last Trumpet, described by Paul in his letter to the Corinthians[2], will be the last blast on the Feast of Trumpets. At this time the dead will be raised and the believers will be lifted up and changed *'in the twinkling of an eye'* to become imperishable.

When Jesus said that *'nobody would know the day nor the hour'* he was using a Hebrew idiom to refer to the uncertainty of the day of the start of the Feast of Trumpets and (thus) the uncertainty of the day when the Bridegroom would come for the Bride. Traditionally the father of the bridegroom chooses the moment that his son was sent to fetch his bride. The Feast starts when the first sliver of the new moon becomes visible, and nobody knows exactly the day or the hour when the new moon starts. Since the Feast of Trumpets is the only feast that starts on the new moon the idiom can easily be clarified. Do you think that the Son really doesn't know about the day and the hour? Jesus and the Father are One, so He knows everything from the beginning.[3] The Hebrew Wedding ritual in the next chapter will explain why the Bridegroom in fact does know but also submits to His Father. Our call is to be watchful, looking for His coming.

---

2   1 Cor. 15: 51-52.
3   John 14:11.

### The Three Themes of the Feast of Trumpets

The Feast of Trumpets is also called Yom Teru'ah, *'The Day of the Wake Up Trumpet.'* It calls everyone to prepare to meet the King of Kings. *'Turn around'*[1], says the Jewish tradition, for the Day of Atonement is coming, but also the Great Day when God will judge.

The three key themes In Judaism are:

1. The Crowning of the King

2. The Wedding of the Messiah

3. The Resurrection of the Dead

Not surprisingly, these Jewish themes are fully in line with the New covenant fulfilment of the Feast of Trumpets:

### 1. The Crowning of the King

The twenty-four elders cast their crowns before the throne at the crowning of the King in heaven.[2] But Christians today are so often taught that God is concerned about their lives and well-being, forgetting the call to die to self. We must learn to serve and worship Jesus in our lives, as we will one day have to give an account. After His coronation, Jesus returns to Jerusalem to defeat the satanic armies and start the Millennium.

### 2. The Wedding Ceremony of the Messiah

The exact time of the Bridegroom coming to retrieve the Bride is unknown (to the Bride), hence the call to the Bride to be always watchful and prepared. After the ceremony the Bride and Bridegroom are not visible for the public since they are in the Bridal room for seven days. Do these seven hidden days portray the seven year tribulation after the Rapture of the Bride of Christ?

### 3. The Resurrection of the Dead

The Talmud and the Machzor, the Jewish book of Prayers for the feast

---

1 Teshuvah.
2 Rev.4:10.

of Trumpets, both indicate the rising of the dead on this Feast day in the future. It was prophesied by Paul that this will happen again at the time of the taking away of the Bride.[3]

## White Clothes

The ancient Jewish tradition is that everyone should wear spotless white clothes during the Feast of Trumpets. During the preparation month of Elul clothes were washed and stretched and folded to be ready for the Feast. This outward removal of dirt was a picture of the cleansing of our souls in preparation for His coming.

The Feast was the day when all work stopped and people put on their white clothes. '*He that overcomes, the same shall be clothed in white raiment, and Jesus Christ shall not blot his name out of the Book of Life.*' [4]This is a daily reminder that we are called to be holy as He is Holy.[5] We cannot claim we have died with Christ and enjoy His resurrection life if we live unsanctified lives. **Only the dead can rise!**

## The Last Trumpet and other Trumpets Clarified

Paul says that the resurrection of the dead will take place at the sound of the Last Trumpet. This has been confused with the seventh trumpet in Revelation 11:15 when, '*The kingdom of the world has become the kingdom of our Lord and of His Messiah*'. But this trumpet is part of a series bringing judgement on the earth, whereas the last trumpet sounded at the Rapture is a joyful call to the Bride!

The Bible mentions three trumpets: **The First Trumpet** was sounded every year at the start of the Feast of Weeks; **The Great Trumpet (Shofar Hagadol)** was sounded at the end of the Day of Atonement when the Gate of Heaven is closed and there will be no further chance to get one's name into the Book of Life. We repeat that Jesus Christ will return to the Mount of Olives on Yom Kippur – the Day of Atonement. **The Last**

---

3   1 Cor. 15:51-52.
4   Rev. 19:8.
5   1 Peter 1:16.

**Trumpet** is connected by Paul with the resurrection of the dead and the taking away of the Bride of Christ and we explained earlier that is the theme of this Feast of Trumpets.

There are five trumpet notes: **The Tekiah**, a long note as a sign of contentment and war; **The Shevarim,** three short notes - a sign of weeping; **The Teru'ah,** nine very short notes as a sign of alarm. These notes are played for 99 notes, then there is the very elongated **Tekiah Gedolah,** the 100th or Last Trumpet, a sign of resurrection, deliverance and the start of the restoration of Israel.

### The Door will be open for a 'short while'

The parable of the Wise and Foolish Virgins,[1] shows that the Bridegroom will evaluate our heart attitudes. Those who have prepared themselves by daily serving Him, represented by the barley harvest, will be welcomed at the Banquet. Those who have been lukewarm spectators will, like the wheat harvest, suffer the bruising of the threshing sledge, the Roman 'tribulum' now called Tribulation. When they turn to Christ in repentance, Revelation says many will be killed by the antichrist.

There is a difference: barley was harvested by repeatedly tossing the grain in the air with a winnowing shovel until the chaff was separated from the barley grain.
The threshing of wheat however was performed by a tribulum, a threshing sledge. As seen in the picture, this was a heavy wooden board with flints embedded on the underside, which was dragged by horses across the wheat. Tribulation comes from the Latin word "tribulum"

1  Matt. 25.

The Talmud also calls the Feast of Trumpets the '**Yom Hakese**', the hidden day. The Wise Virgins will be hidden from the tribulation as the Jews were hidden from the later plagues in the Land of Goshen. The Jews say to each other at the Feast, '*May you be written in the Book of Life.*'

The Talmud also calls the Feast the '**Yom HaDin**' – the Day of Judgement. According to tradition God will open three books for the living and those who died: the books of the righteous, the unrighteous and the in-between group. The New Testament helps us to see these groups in relation to His Coming. The righteous will be raptured and will meet Him in the air; the lukewarm will be tested during the seven year Tribulation on earth, to see if they will now stand up for their faith, possibly as martyrs; and finally the unrighteous who will be judged at the end of the Millennium. But today '*The time has come for judgement to begin at the house of God.*'[2]

The Feast of Trumpets calls us to put our lives in order to prepare for the Bridegroom. **Understanding the Feasts helps us to have oil in our lamps and live a life of sanctification and of proclaiming the gospel.**

**Day of Atonement – Yom Kippur**
This day is the climax following the season of Repentance for believers, not for outsiders. It is the day when the people of God humble themselves deeply before God and are cleansed of sin by God's mercy. **It is the most sacred day of the year in Israel.** The High Priest and the Sanctuary were cleansed by the blood of a bull and the "goat for the Lord" whose body was taken outside the camp. This is the reason that Jesus was crucified outside the city. After cleansing the sanctuary with the blood, the High Priest transferred all the sins of the nation by laying his hands on the scapegoat that was **not** for the Lord. The blood of this goat was **not** shed to cleanse. Instead the goat was taken outside the camp and thrown off a cliff[3]. This was to be sure it never returned, just as satan will be thrown into the abyss for a 1000 years, after which he will end up

---

2   1 Pet. 4:17.
3   According to Jewish tradition.

in the lake of fire and sulphur.[1] The original Biblical thought was that the scapegoat was the origin of all evil who will eventually have this evil come back on his head.

**The Reason for the Day of Atonement**

The Pesach (Passover) message is that we were freed from the bondage of sin. The application of His blood on our "doorposts" is the condition for death passing over. We have to obey, but salvation is pure Grace by faith. Then at Sinai we entered into a bi-lateral covenant with God and joined His congregation (Pentecost). But it is the strong and holy God who joined with the weak man who tends to transgress. Some orthodox Protestants have said that our weakness means we can never be sure we are a child of God. But God says He will overcome our weakness by the power of the indwelling Holy Spirit who enables New Covenant believers to be able to mortify the flesh.[2] Our weakness is the very reason He created a Covenant with His people, it was not our worthiness that caused it.

Reconciliation in the Old Testament was not 'imperfect', since Christ had died since the foundation of the world to put the names of the redeemed in the Book of Life.[3] In the sacrificial system an innocent life was given for a guilty life – a shadow of Calvary - one of the most important principles in the Bible. But in the New Covenant it is not enough just to say, '*Sorry*.' What matters is the condition of our hearts and the deeds that follow. The veil of the Temple may have been torn, but we still have a High Priest in heaven as a Mediator for repentant believers.

**Deliverance and judicial forgiveness at Pesach are for those who were not yet cleansed and delivered, but fatherly forgiveness and reconciliation are for those already delivered who sin afterwards and need a restoration of their relationship within an existing covenant. In the New covenant the Day of Atonement is still an everlasting feast, but**

1  Gen. 3:15, Rev. 20:10.
2  Rom. 8:2,13.
3  Rev. 13:8.

**it is to be celebrated the whole year around, since our High Priest will never leave us or forsake us.**

Moses went twice up Mount Sinai into the Holy of Holies – God's Presence – to bring God's forgiveness and atonement to the people. The second coming of Moses took place on the Day of Atonement, a shadow of Jesus Christ who will come a second time on the last great Day of Atonement. What the High Priest did once a year in the Holy of Holies is now done continuously by our heavenly High Priest Christ Jesus, the Mediator of a better covenant. As a minister of the sanctuary and of the true tabernacle, our Advocate brings reconciliation between God the Father and the covenantal believer who repents.[4]

### God's relationship with the Believer on the Way

We can look at time as a straight line but also as a series of cycles that show that failure is not the end because a new beginning follows. The failure of mankind at the Flood led to a new beginning with Noah. The present failure also has a new beginning in the Millennium. God seeks to reconcile with mankind time and again.

In Revelation we see that there is a final Sabbath cycle of seven years – in which we see seven seals broken, seven trumpets blown and seven vials poured out before the return of the Messiah.

We often hear that God remembers our sins no more – but this relates to the past at the time of our conversion. It does not apply thereafter unless our hearts are first humbled by confession to attract God's forgiveness. This allows the cycle of failure being followed by a new start to operate. But at each circle we are expected to rise to a higher level of maturity so as to 'walk as Jesus walked.'[5]

We come to know God better as Master, King and Father when we learn to trust him even when we feel betrayed as Job did. 'Though He slay me,

---

4   Heb. 8, 1 John 1:9, 2:1.
5   1 John 2:6.

*yet will I trust Him.*[1] It all worked out for Job, and it will for us, as we learn to use our testing times to become more fruitful. Jesus warned of many tribulations on the road from Pesach (His crucifixion and resurrection and our redemption) to the fulfilment of the Day of Atonement (His Return).[2]

### The Pesach Sacrifice as a Substitute Sin Offering?

Jews, who do not believe in Yeshua as the Messiah, may have a problem when Christians tell them that Yeshua was a *Sin* Offering, since Passover (Pesach) was a *Peace* Offering because the person offering the sacrifice ate the sacrificial lamb. But Yeshua's role as an offering was linked to *all* the other feasts so that His blood was related to the Peace Offering of Pesach, the animal offerings in the sacrificial system and the Sin Offering of the Day of Atonement.

The Church has concentrated on the Gospel as the forgiveness of sin on Passover, having lost the meaning of all the seven feasts. But the blood of Jesus Christ also has deep meaning for the Day of Atonement since He entered the heavenly Sanctuary as High Priest with His own blood to bring reconciliation when we repent as Christians and ask forgiveness.

### The Meanings of Pesach and the Day of Atonement in our lives

Christians often see the Torah as the Law from which we have been delivered in Christ. But 'Simchat Torah', on the next day after the Feast of Tabernacles, is when Jews celebrate the lamp of the Torah as the guide for their lives. They sing and dance, carrying the Torah round the Synagogue in a procession.

The Feasts show that we have judicial forgiveness in relation to **Pesach** through the blood of Jesus, and fatherly reconciliation that continuously restores our relationship with God in relation to the (continuous) **Day of Atonement**. Hence the need to live as unleavened bread without sin. If we persist in combining the world with our walk as Christians there will

---

1   Job 13:15.
2   Acts 14:22.

be no 'passing over' and we will be cut off from the community. We start our life of faith with **redemption** as a sovereign act of God at Pesach; then we work out our **salvation** through the desert journey of our lives as we learn to obey the Word and the Spirit, walking the Law of Christ; this ultimately brings us to **glorification** in the 'Promised Land'.

### The Condition to Participate in the Day of Atonement

Christians can have a misunderstanding as to why Jesus died. Was it because God is righteous and cannot look upon sin? Do we have a wrathful God of the Old Testament and a loving Son of the New Testament who paid the penalty and restored a relationship that we could not accomplish ourselves? This overlooks the fact **that God is One and that He Himself took the initiative** to recover His family because He loves us so much He would even die for us.

The Feasts show us that we have victory over death and satan through faith in the blood of the Lamb; that is freedom from slavery and liberation from the kingdom of darkness; an atoning sacrifice and a ransom paid to enter a new covenant and become a spotless Bride and fully enter a great inheritance in the Millennium. **All this came not from an angry God, but from a loving Father who yearned for His prodigal family to be restored to Him.**

### Do We Still Need Sacrifices today?

A sacrifice is usually associated with penance and forgiveness. But the Jews also gave voluntary burnt offerings as a sign of their gratitude and devotion. A sacrifice reflects our heart condition, whether we love God enough to obey Him. *'I desire love and not sacrifice, the knowledge of God rather than a burnt offering.'* [3]The sacrificial system of the Old Covenant has been ended, but our love for God will still produce such daily spiritual sacrifices as praise, helping the poor, and visiting the sick.[4] And it

---

3  Hos. 6:6.
4  1 Pet.2:5.

67

should all be related to the Sacrifice of Jesus Christ, who gave His life, so we might live. We offer our bodies as living sacrifices.[1]

### The Day of Atonement – The reality in Christ

For Christians, daily confession of sins should be normal, because the blood of Jesus Christ is still being applied for the repentant sinner in the Heavenly Temple. Jesus was himself a spotless sacrifice for sin, and He gave himself as a sin **offering** for us, that we might receive His righteousness.[2]

### Ongoing Repentance and Mediation

It is a mistake to say that we are only in the age of grace since the Resurrection of Jesus Christ. We have seen that grace was always central to the Old Testament – God does not change. It was God's grace that forgave David, after the murder of Uriah, because God saw what was in his heart. This should comfort those who have been taught to fear for their salvation. The High Priest is always in the Heavens attending to the cry of their hearts.[3]

Some Liberal thinkers now suggest that, as Jesus has died for our sins, that none of their deeds are any longer regarded as sins, although they are according to the Law of Christ. From now on, 'it's all about grace'. But Paul asks if we are to continue to sin that grace may abound? '*May it never be!*' he replies.[4] If we have died to sin and were baptized into His death, can we still live in sin?

We should not be anxious that our sins are still with us after repentance, nor should we presume that they are forgiven and forgotten by God without repentance. God does look at our heart, but He wants us to confess with our lips. The blood of Jesus was at Calvary, and has been ever since, available to us. If we confess our sins God is faithful to

---

1  Rom. 12:1.
2  2 Cor. 5:8.
3  Heb. 8:1.
4  Rom. 6:2.

forgive our sins, and if we say we have not sinned we make God a liar.[5] John is talking here to believers!

## Does sin still have consequences?

When we confess any sin and ask for forgiveness, they are forgiven. But it is important not to hide our sins, or minimise their significance to God. We are also required to ask the offended person for forgiveness and repay, where possible, the damage we have done. The Bible provides clear guidelines for this. We need to have a hatred of sin, and to apply the meaning of the Feast of Unleavened Bread daily.

## The Day of Atonement in the New Covenant and in the Future

Jesus Christ has entered the Heavenly Temple with His blood, but His work of cleansing us from sin continues until the final Day of Atonement when He leaves the Heavenly Temple to be seen by all the tribes of Israel to show that their reconciliation with God has taken place. Then those broken branches of the Olive Tree that are the 'refined' will be grafted back in. So the seventieth week of years will be completed when transgression will be finished and sin will have been brought to an end, as was foretold in the book Daniel. [6]

## The Return of Jesus and the Day of Atonement

Before Jesus returns at the Mount of Olives, there will be a seven year period of increasing tribulation. The Antichrist-system will require everyone to be marked and without this mark no one can buy or sell. Jerusalem will be conquered, there will be many martyrs and such terrible judgements of God that mankind would be wiped out unless God cuts short His wrath for the sake of the Elect.

Jesus, on His return, will destroy the satanic armies at Armageddon and remove the veil so that all nations will know Him. There will be the Millennial 1000 years of peace on earth. At the end of this Great Sabbath,

---

5   1 John 1:9-10. Heb. 4:15-16.
6   Dan. 9:24. Zech. 13:9.

satan will be released for a short period of time to deceive the nations again before his final defeat. He will then be cast into the lake of fire. Then the new Heaven and Earth will come with the Heavenly Jerusalem.[1]

### The Day of Atonement and the Feast of Trumpets

The Feast of Trumpets pictures the taking away in the air of the Bride of Christ by the Bridegroom. The Day of Atonement is the celebration of the return of the Messiah as King to Jerusalem. This will be the High Priest coming out of the Heavenly tabernacle and unto them that look for Him shall He appear the second time without sin unto salvation.[2] The world will see Him and all the remnant of Israel will be saved. The seven year tribulation is mirrored by the seven full days between the end of the Feasts of Trumpets (Tishri 1-2) and the day of Atonement (Tishri 9, after sunset), but also by the bridal week in relation to the Hebrew wedding ritual as will be explained in the next chapter.

### Daniel's Last Week of Years and the Day of Atonement

Daniel was told the exact number of days (years) for the periods of history. The last week of years is likely to begin on the Feast of Trumpets and will end seven years later, on the Day of Atonement. Then the period of abomination will end, and there will be everlasting righteousness.[3]

### Will Messiah Return in a Jubilee Year? – the seven cycles

Each fiftieth year is a Jubilee Year. It is a year of restoration after seven periods of seven years. These cycles of sevens are evident in the times of history that God has sovereignly determined. When we come to the Book of Revelation we see seven smaller cycles within a larger cycle of the seven year Tribulation Period. Seven seals are opened, and out of the seventh seal comes seven trumpets, the seventh trumpet leads to seven plagues. And finally the seventh plague produces the cry, 'It is done!'

---

1  Rev. 21.
2  Heb. 9:28.
3  Dan. 9:24.

## Unrolling the Scroll of 7s

There is a mathematical structure to the Book of Revelation. A large circle of seven years contains seven smaller circles of seven seals; the central circle has the seventh seal linked to the start of seven trumpets; the seventh trumpet releases seven plagues before Messiah comes. This implies that the three circles of each six circles are incomplete – they are in fact only 666 – until the final cry, 'It *is done*', when all circles will be complete at the same time – 777![4]  A circle also has 360 degrees. When we multiply x 7 we come to the number 2520 and this is the number we also know from the books of Daniel and Revelation. All this shows God's complete control of time – He knows the end from the beginning!

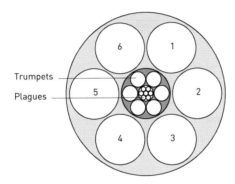

## Feast of tabernacles – Sukkot

The Feast of Tabernacles starts in the 7th month on the 14th of Tishri after sunset (= start 15th of Tishri) and is celebrated for 7 days. It looks back to the days that they lived in booths in the desert and that Moses began to build the Tabernacle in the wilderness. God had chosen to dwell among His Covenant people. But it also reminds us that we are only sojourners on Earth as we wait for the New Jerusalem. Because of our gratitude at receiving Divine forgiveness[5], **Tabernacles is a feast of great rejoicing!**

---

4  Rev. 16:17.
5  see the New Covenant reality of the Day of Atonement in Christ.

### Israel Restored as a Nation of Mediators

The final Day of Atonement will bring reconciliation to **all the tribes of Israel** with each other and with God. Then the fulfilment of the Feast of Tabernacles will be the Feast of true reconciliation and joy for all nations. It is the start of the Millennium and from then on, every year, all nations will go up to Jerusalem for Tabernacles, and Israel will be a royal priesthood for all the nations of the earth.

### End of the Harvest

In Israel, everyone is happy at Tabernacles because the harvest is brought in. But with barns full of barley, wheat, fruit and olives God tells them to live in booths for a time, to remind them who the Source of Life really is. New covenant believers, are called to remember all His blessings and to focus on the One who will reign in Jerusalem during the Millennium and who will provide a real and durable house in the New Jerusalem.

### Jesus' Birth and the Feast of Tabernacles

Jesus was born almost certainly on the first day of Tabernacles and circumcised on the eighth day, both days were High Sabbaths. Because of the crowds come up for the Feast, Jesus was born in Bethlehem in a Tabernacle booth built for the Feast, since there was no place in the Inn.

The shepherds of Bethlehem were educated Levites shepherding the lambs for the Temple sacrifices. They knew the Feast of Tabernacles was the Feast of Joy for all nations. So they very well understood the angelic message, *'tidings of **great joy** which will be to **all people'***, foretelling the coming of One Who would come to bring great Joy.[1] In every booth there was a wooden bread basket with linen cloths to keep the bread fresh. We can see how Jesus was wrapped in and where He lay – a bread basket! He is the Bread of Life and was born in Beth-lehem, which means the 'House of Bread!'. All this is very different from the pagan way we celebrate the birth of Jesus today instituted from the 4th century AD. Should we not follow God's pattern?

---

1   Luke 2:10.

### The Ceremony in which Water was Poured out

At Sukkot the Jews remembered God's provision of water in the wilderness when Moses struck the Rock.[2] Water from the well of Siloam was taken through the Watergate to be poured out with the blood of the sacrifice. Now let's put the words of Jesus into context. As this was happening Jesus cried out, *'If anyone thirsts, let him come to me and drink. He who believes in me, ... out of his mouth will flow rivers of living water'.*[3] Equally so, Jesus was referring to the fact that He was the spiritual Rock that had travelled with them in the desert. [4]

### Light of the World

At dawn at Tabernacles a priest lit large candlesticks about 25 meters high in the Temple court, visible to most of Jerusalem, to remind them of the Pillar of Fire in the desert. When Jesus said, *'I am the Light of the World. Whoever follows me will never walk in darkness but he will have the Light of life'*[5], He linked the candlesticks with Himself.

### Are we ordered to be joyful?

God indeed ordered to celebrate this feast with joy[6] and there is a reason for that. The feast of Tabernacles remembers that God was about to withdraw His protection from the Jews after they worshipped the golden calf until Moses, as a type of Christ, interceded for them. But after great remorse and some judgement God ordered the building of the Tabernacle to dwell with them. What Joy! The Joy is also because New covenant believers expect Him to return and dwell with them forever. What JOY!

### Tabernacles in Prophecy for the End of the Sixth Day

Zechariah 14 is read during Sukkot. Christians realise that it tells of the final battle when Jesus comes to defeat the armies of the nations attacking Jerusalem. Then in the thousand years of peace that follows, the Feast of Tabernacles will be kept at Jerusalem. Those nations who do not

---

2  Ex. 17:6.
3  John 7:37-38.
4  1 Cor. 10:4.
5  John 8:12.
6  Deut. 16:15-15.

go up will receive no rain, showing that there may still be disobedience under the reign of Christ.

### Celebrating the New Feast of Tabernacles in Jerusalem?

Should we go up Jerusalem to celebrate the Feast? While this would be a great experience, God tells us[1] to celebrate where He chooses to abide. Since we have become temples of the Holy Spirit,[2] He abides in us, so we can congregate anywhere to celebrate with joy. He is the Source of living water and the Light of this world and He wants to dwell in us. We are His tabernacles!

### The Jews, like the Gentiles, also Forgot the Feasts

When King Josiah came to power the Feasts had not been celebrated since Samuel.[3] The prophet Ezra also had to restore the feast of Tabernacles.[4] The Church also stopped celebrating the Feasts from the 3rd century. In essence, both Jews and Gentiles, through disobedience, both sank into unbelief and idolatry. Only now are we returning to these rehearsals that help us to be disciples from a pure heart. Not only do we understand that He is the Way but also He gave a way, illustrated by the pattern of the Feasts, for every believer.

### Can we Choose our Own Feasts?

Messianic Jews and Messianic Gentiles are co-heirs through the New Covenant and are all called to participate in the prophetic Feasts in their New Covenant significance. When Paul told the Galatians not to observe days, months, times and years he was talking about the *pagan* practices they were falling back to.[5]

### The Seven Feasts as Phases in the Life of Every Christian

Just to summarise: the three **Spring Feasts** reflect deliverance & cleansing, peace with God by faith, the rejection of sin and the desire to obey

---

1   In Deut. 16:6
2   1 Cor. 3:16,
3   2 Kings 23:22.
4   Ezra 3:4.
5   Gal. 4:8-10.

God and to be a new creation. The central Feast of **Pentecost** reflects the need for the power of the Holy Spirit with His fruit, gifts, boldness and armour. This enables us to walk as Jesus walked with the blessing of His Covenant and the power of His Spirit. Then the dry, testing summer follows before the Bride's wedding celebration and before we enter our Promised Land.

### A Delicate Matter: Living a Jewish or non-Jewish Life

For those who have put on Christ after their salvation by faith, there is now neither Jew nor Greek.[6] That does not mean that Messianic Jews have to abandon their Jewish roots. One thing however is certain: Christians and Messianic Jews will always find each other in the New Covenant meanings of the shadows and patterns originally portrayed in the Old Covenant. We need to see that 'Jewish' Feasts are equally Christian Feasts. Once we are liberated from our false Greco-Roman roots, from many Roman Catholic and Protestant traditions, and from current Postmodernist theology, we can re-discover the purity of the early Church. There are different branches in the Olive Tree – so there is no need to unlovingly disconnect from other branches. All circumcised of heart are children of Abraham, branches of the same Olive Tree of which Yeshua is the root. Celebrating the feasts is **not** about the ritual. We need to understand how to live out the meaning of these feasts in our daily walk as disciples of Yeshua.

### How Christians should discern Biblical Feasts and Judaism

On one hand, some Jews want to underline that celebrating the Feasts does not make you Jewish nor do they want Christians to grasp the rituals of Judaism while ignoring the Law of Moses.

On the other hand, most Christians have been brought up to ignore the Feasts as associated with Judaism & the Mosaic Law. But now they are discovering Christ in the Old Testament and the value of the Feasts to their spiritual growth. They are also looking forward to Christ fulfilling

---

6  Gal. 3:28.

the Fall Feasts at His Second Coming. Messianic Jews keep the Feasts already in their Covenant meaning, so they can really be bridges.

Knowledge of the Feasts will equip Christians to show Jews that Messiah Yeshua is the Key to understanding their Scriptures. One day, when the veil is removed and all of Israel is re-rooted in the Olive Tree, all nations will be taught by God's Chosen People, then restored to glory.[1]

1   Is. 60:1-3.

# Chapter Six

# THE ANCIENT WEDDING CEREMONY

The ancient Hebrew wedding ceremony is revelatory in explaining the Heavenly Wedding of Scripture and was well known to the disciples of Jesus. The Bible calls Jesus the Bridegroom and the Body of Christ is the Bride. The Hebrew wedding background will stir up our desire to be spotless and eager to meet the Bridegroom! The Wedding process is as follows:

### The Matchmaker

The father would usually employ a matchmaker to go out and find a bride who matched the profile provided by the father. As an example, Abraham sent Eliezer to find a wife for Isaac, who had agreed to the mission. Rebecca also agreed to the proposed marriage.

After the prospective bride had been found, a meeting was arranged in a neutral place like at the well. If there was affection between the couple, the next step was for the bridegroom to visit the home of his future bride. It was important that both Bride and Bridegroom made their own decisions.

### The Bridegroom's First Visit

Then the bridegroom comes with his father to the house of the bride. The bridegroom has the cup of the covenant, the wine, and the ransom or dowry with him. The father of the bride asks his daughter for permission to open the door when there is a knock. If the future bride likes the boy, she agrees and the door is opened so that he and his father can enter for a meal prepared by the bride. This is the start of negotiations for the marriage, as Jesus said:

> *Behold, I stand at the door and knock. If anyone hears My voice and opens the door, I will come in to him and dine with him, and he with me.*[1]

### The Bridegroom gives the Bride His Marriage Contract

The marriage contract, the 'ketubah', is a legal document with the obligations of the bridegroom to protect and provide security for the bride.

---

1  Rev. 3:20.

From the moment an agreement is reached, the bride has an inheritance even though the wedding has not yet taken place, as we have our inheritance in Christ before the marriage of the Lamb has come.[1]

The Torah is the 'ketubah' that God gave to His people on Mount Sinai who all agreed, saying, *'All the words which the Lord has said, we will do.'*[2] The bride's response is to set herself completely apart, as the Jews became God's chosen and separate people. This is called the sanctification of the bride. Similarly Christians have been bought and paid for and they are no longer their own.[3] The Torah was never considered as a Law given to make us stumble, but as guidelines for a God-fearing and therefore a good life. It was the wedding document. Equally, the new covenant believer obeys His commandments and in doing so fulfils the Law of Christ because he loves Him.

### The Bridegroom Acquires his Bride by Paying a Dowry

The price paid by the bridegroom shows how valuable he thinks the bride is. This reminding us of the price paid by Jesus to set us free from the world and the devil and to provide an inheritance. With this payment the bride is set aside from her family for a reason, reminding us that we are still in the world, but no longer of the world. Likewise new covenant believers cannot daily apply the enormous sacrifice of His precious blood on the doorposts of their lives without submitting daily to *all* of His Word. They have been bought at a price and are no longer their own.[4]

### The Bride Becomes Exclusive to the Groom

By entering the *ketubah* the bride legally becomes his wife, although she does not live with her husband yet. We are also legally wed to Christ, but we have not yet joined Him. The *ketubah* stipulates that the bride is a virgin, and will keep herself pure, just as the Bride of Christ seeks with His help to be spotless and untainted by the world. Jesus has offered us

---

1  Rev. 3:7-9.
2  Ex. 24:3.
3  1 Cor. 6:19-20.
4  1 Cor. 6:19-20. Eph. 1:14.

His atonement, security and protection, but to be received daily by the heart rather than a spoken formula.

### Sealing of the Betrothal by the Cup of Wine

When the *ketubah* is signed, the groom offers a cup of wine to the bride which they drink together with a spoken solemn commitment as a sign they have entered the covenant **together**. The bridegroom then says, '*I will not drink of this cup until we are reunited.*' We can now understand the words of Jesus:

> *"Then He took the cup, and gave thanks, and gave it to them, saying,*
> *'Drink from it, all of you. For this is my blood of the new covenant,*
> *which is shed for many for the remission of sins. But I say to you,*
> *I will not drink of this fruit of the vine from now on until the day*
> *when I drink it new in My Father's kingdom'".*[5]

These words of Jesus were clearly tied to the wedding ceremony and the *ketubah* of the New Covenant. Every time we have Communion and drink the cup we can remember:

- this is part of the Pesach feast as a sign of deliverance and sanctification by the death and resurrection of Yeshua.

- that this cup belongs to His body broken for sinners with the Blood Covenant that will lead to the Marriage Covenant on that great heavenly wedding Day.

- that Messianic believers from the Gentiles have become co-heirs with the originally Israelite bride.

### The Bridegroom Give Gifts to the Bride

The bridegroom does not leave the bride until he has given her gifts, apart from the cup, to honour her and to remind her of his love until they meet again. So the Holy Spirit was poured out at the Feast of Weeks

5 Matt. 26:27.

81

as a gift, a Helper, following the seder meal (last supper) that also took place with the disciples in a wedding context. The Holy Spirit has come to write His law on our hearts and to sanctify us as His own so that we can meet the Bridegroom at the great day of the Rapture as kindred spirits. But He is also the Comforter and the Teacher until the time of the return of the Bridegroom.

### The Bridegroom Leaves to Prepare a Place

While the betrothal was a public affair at the bride's house, the marriage was going to be at the bridegroom's father's house for invited guests only. While we are publicly betrothed to the heavenly Bridegroom, our wedding also will be restricted to those invited by God.[1] But after the sealing of the betrothal, the bridegroom leaves the bride to prepare a room for his bride in his father's house, something the disciples under-stood when Jesus said,

> 'In my Father's house are many mansions; if it were not so, I would have told you. I go to prepare a place for you. And if I go and prepare a place for you, I will come again and receive you to Myself; that where I am, there you may be also.'[2]

When Jesus left at (what we now call) Ascension Day He had much work to do in heaven interceding for us daily as our Advocate so that His bride will be pure when He comes to fulfil the fifth Feast of Trumpets. He is already preparing a place for all the saints!

### Veiled

On his departure, the bridegroom places a veil over the bride to show that she belongs to him, just as we call ourselves Christians to show we are committed to our Bridegroom. This time of preparation led Jesus to say: 'A little while, and you will not see Me; and again a little while, and you will see Me.'[3]

---

1  Rev. 19:9.
2  John 14:2.
3  John 16:16.

**The Bride Uses the Separation Time Well**
The bride is very busy in the time between when the bridegroom leaves and the wedding day, just as New Covenant Believers also have similar work to do. There are 3 focal points for the bride:

**1. The Bride Purifies and Prepares herself**
The Hebrew bride has purification rituals in water (*mikveh*). This immersion is the same word as for baptism, just as Paul talks about spiritual cleansing.[4] During the absence of the groom she also weaves her wedding garment, just as believers, though their righteous deeds, weave their wedding garment as a response to their election.[5] This has nothing to do with justification, but sanctification with the help of the Holy Spirit. It is because we have a deep desire to please Him who first loved us! The Bride is warned that spiritual adultery is enmity with the Bridegroom.[6]
There is a delay waiting for the wedding day, just as there is also a long dry summer leading up to the autumn feasts, and a long period of testing in the wilderness before Israel reached the Promised Land. These trials, if we are overcomers, lead to a deeper relationship with God and more responsibility later.
In world history we have arrived in "the month of Elul", a time of repentance and preparation, because the harvest is approaching and the Promised Land is in sight. Many Churches have been infected by postmodern or humanistic thinking. However there is a smaller group, the Bible speaks of a remnant, seeking purity of heart with expectant prayer and the good works that He has prepared for them as they await the Bridegroom.
Pastors now have an important role in fighting the spirit of the age and teaching the earthly marriage in the light of the heavenly reality. They have to resist the thinking that the world has changed and we need to go along with its immorality. Young couples, who are taught the Hebrew

4   1 Cor. 6:11.
5   Rev. 19:8.
6   James 4:4.

foundation for marriage and the parallel with Christ and His Body, can more easily obey and reflect God's Word in society.

## 2. The Bride Weaves Tapestries for the Future House

The bride, in response to the love of the bridegroom who has made her a joint-heir of his estate, weaves tapestries to decorate their new home in his father's house. This is a picture of the righteous acts of the saints who are clothed in fine linen.[1]

When the bride arrives in her new home her tapestries will be appraised. This is the judgement seat of Christ for believer's works. If they have been done in obedience to the Holy Spirit for the glory of God, they will be valued as gold, silver or precious stones. If not these works will burn in the fire like wood, hay or straw.[2] As believers express their love in good works, guided by His Spirit, they become Ambassadors of Christ, a royal priesthood, a holy nation.

## 3. Vigilant Expectation of the Arrival of the Bridegroom

Sometimes the bride had to wait one or two years, as the groom was busy building their home and the bridal room in his father's house. This reminds us of the two thousand years waiting for Messiah to return. When news got out that the home was almost built, ten unmarried girl friends of the bride would wait outside at dusk alongside the road. There were no streetlights in that time and that is why the virgins needed to have their lights shining. The bridegroom always came in the evening so that they were home before midnight. This reflects the Rapture before the darkest time when God will have to judge the antichrist and all that have chosen to follow him.

The Bride's real home is the Bridegroom's house, which she hadn't seen until that moment. That is a shadow of what the Bible says:

---

1  Rev. 19:8.
2  1 Cor. 3:12-13.

*'Eye has not seen, nor ear heard, nor have entered into the heart of man,
the things which God has prepared for those who love Him.'*[3]

The Feast of Trumpets, which is all about the taking away of the Bride,
starts at night when the new moon first appears. Jesus told His disciples
the story of slaves awaiting their master. They should have their waists
girded and their lamps burning, a picture of the readiness of believers.
Then, when the Master comes, amazingly He bends down to serve His
servants during a meal![4]

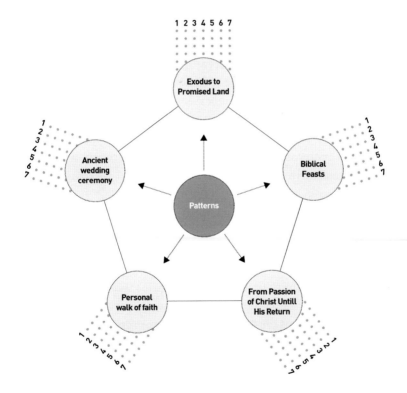

### The Bride is in This World, but Not of It

Some Churches have withdrawn to 'protect themselves' from the world with like-minded believers, but this is not in line with the picture that the Bride is showing in the Wedding ceremony; others believe we are called to be in the world and partake of the world wholeheartedly. We may struggle to plot the right Biblical course within this field of tension, but the ritual of the Wedding ceremony may be of help. The Bride wears a veil to show that she is betrothed, but she continues in society, and is glad to speak about her bridegroom. We are also commanded to waste no opportunity to preach the Gospel.[1]

Although we are preparing and waiting for the Great Wedding Day, we will not establish the Kingdom on earth until the King returns. We have been established by deliverance and justification at Pesach, we remove sin from our walk and live as unleavened bread, we have been resurrected to a newness of life as pictured by First Fruits and we are called to obedience to Word and Spirit as we walk in covenant with God, made possible at Pentecost. We are disciples, clothed in armour, who will be able to withstand in the evil day, and having done all, we stand until the Bridegroom comes.[2]

### What Are Our Priorities?

The last generation before the Bridegroom's return needs a passion for discipleship in every area of life, not just following a Church programme or traditions. But the Church also needs to spring into action and do the Word of God, because, as James says, faith without works is dead. Faith without actions turns the Gospel into cold theory and does not make us a follower of Christ.

### The Bridegroom Does not Know When He May Return for the Bride

The father of the groom decides when the house is ready. When Jesus said that 'only the Father knows'[3], He was giving a guarded referral to the wedding for those who have ears to hear and expectant hearts.

---

1  2 Tim. 4:2.
2  Eph. 6:13.
3  Matt. 24:36.

## The Bridegroom Departs for the Bride

When the father has given permission for the bride to be fetched, the groom's best friend runs ahead and blows the Shofar to alert the bridesmaids that the coming of the bridegroom is at hand. This reflects the Feast of Trumpets that is about the coming of Messiah and the raising of the dead at the *last trumpet*.[4] It is also, to use a Jewish idiom, at the **exact** time (of the new moon) that no one knows, except the Father.

## The Bridegroom Snatches the Bride Away

When the Shofar sounds, everything happens very quickly – there is no more time for the bride to prepare. The groom does not enter the bride's house, but snatches her away at the doorstep. Likewise, at the Rapture, we will meet Jesus on our threshold in the clouds, in the twinkling of an eye. Everything points to the bride being taken at the Feast of Trumpets, before the days of awe of the seven year tribulation.

## The Official Wedding Ceremony

Tradition tells that when the groom arrives at the bride's house he lifts her up into a carriage, and from that moment her feet no longer touch the earth. The wedding takes place under a *Chupah*, a canopy supported by four wooden poles, symbolic of the groom's protective covering of the bride, just as the pillar of cloud was a protective covering for Israel in the wilderness.

When the bridegroom arrives, he is welcomed with the words,

> *'Blessed is he who has come', just as Jesus said about His return, 'For I say unto you, you shall not see me until you shall say: Blessed is he that comes in the name of the Lord.'*[5]

## Earthly Marriage

The earthly marriage should follow the divine pattern. But people value their independence. Some wives do not submit to the loving authority of

---

4   1 Cor. 15:52, 2 Thess. 4:13-18.
5   Matt. 23:39.

their husband so that the husband cannot enter into his God-given position. Some husbands do not fulfil their God given command to love their
wives as Christ loves His Church. So they both may disobey the divine
commandment and the blessing that goes with it for both partners. Our
enemy has been trying to destroy marriage; to the extent he succeeds
the Church and society will pay for it spiritually, socially and materially.

**The Bridal Chamber**
The bride and groom spend seven days in the bridal chamber, then they
come out for the marriage supper. The bride of Christ and Messiah will
also spend seven years together in heaven before the wedding banquet,
while trouble covers the earth. As it is written:

> 'Come, my people, go into your chambers and shut the doors behind you:
> hide yourselves as it were for a little moment, until the indignation has
> passed. For, behold, the Lord comes out of His place to punish the inhabi-
> tants of the earth for their iniquities.'[1]

In the heavenly Bridal Chamber the Bride, no longer veiled, will see
Yeshua face to face and share His glory, as Adam and Eve had His glory
before the Fall of mankind.[2]

**The Bride and Bridegroom Come Outside**
This is a picture of the end of the seventy weeks of Daniel, when all the
invited Saints share the Banquet as mentioned in the book of Revelation.[3]

**The Marriage Supper and the End of the Wedding**
The Hebrew wedding ceremony shows that the Rapture will be seven
'days' (years) before the Wedding Supper. This time of spiritual fellow-
ship between Bride and Groom will equip the Bride to reign with her
Groom for 1000 years.

---

1  Is. 26: 20-21.
2  1 Cor. 13:12.
3  Rev. 19:9.

### The Bridegroom Takes the Bride to His House

The couple did not stay in the Groom's father's house forever, because the Groom had also built a new house for His bride. In the same way, when Jesus comes back with His Bride, they will reign on earth during the Millennium. Since the Bride will have a glorified body she may at the same time reside in Heaven as well. Jesus will ride as a King on a horseback to defeat the nations deceived by satan with an army including the Saints, all dressed in white.[4]

### The Connection between the Marriage and the Biblical Feasts

The wedding ritual and the Biblical feasts reinforce each other in revealing God's plan and the correct order of events. The long dry summer of 2000 years is almost over and the time has come for the Last Trumpet and the completion of the harvest. Then will come the joy of the Feast of Tabernacles for all nations.

### The Wedding of Bride and Bridegroom Has Not Yet Taken Place

When a person turns to God their life changes completely. The new believer also has a new desire to be at the Wedding with the overcomers of all generations. Through many trials Christ is formed in us, so that Paul writes:

> *'For I am jealous over you with godly jealousy: for I have espoused you to one husband, that I may present you as a chaste virgin to Christ'.*[5]

### Who is the Bride?

Some think that the Church has replaced the Jews to become the new Israel of God. But Paul tells us not to be arrogant towards the Jews who will be grafted back in to the Olive Tree.[6] God has always wanted a covenant people from Adam to Noah to Abraham and with all circumcised of heart who in faith have accepted Jesus as their Saviour and walk accordingly. **There has only ever been one Bride in God's sight.**

---

4  Rev. 17:14, 19:11-16.
5  2 Cor. 11:2.
6  Rom. 11.

## The Fullness of the Bride

The Body of Christ today has the task of teaching all nations and the Jews that Yeshua is the Messiah and coming Bridegroom. Very soon God will show the remnant of Israel still outside the New Covenant that He has not deserted them when He defeats the army of Antichrist that comes against them. This remnant of Israel & Judah will be grafted back in as God promised,[1] and then the Olive Tree will be complete in all its fullness. When the false christ and the false prophet appear, there will also be a false olive tree in which all religions can participate so that a false bride can be presented to the world. We need the Spirit of discernment to keep us in the Truth and to keep our lamps filled with oil.

## When the Church is Not Watchful

In the Song of Solomon there is a terrible warning. The Bride is warned to catch the little foxes that spoil the vineyard. Then the Bride sings, 'My beloved is mine and I am His.'[2] Be aware of the order in this Song. The Bride seems to have become self-centred so that when the Bridegroom calls at night, she does not want to get up! And when she does and opens the door, He is gone. Too late she looks for Him in the city and is beaten by the watchmen. Eventually she knows her place, 'I am my beloved's'.[3] Is this a warning for the generation that sees the Lord's return? Are we lukewarm, self-centred and complacent?[4]

## Similar Shadows – A Firm Anchor

The core purpose of **Wake Up!** is not actually to explain the End Times, but a demonstration that God's Plan of Salvation and Restoration can be seen in five themes or patterns that confirm each other over and again:

1. The Journey of the Exodus from Egypt to the Promised Land.

2. The events of the Passion Week of Christ until His final return.

---

1  Dan. 9:24,
2  Song of S. 2:4.
3  Song of S. 7:10.
4  Rev. 3:16.

3. The New Covenant meaning of each of the seven Biblical Feasts.

4. The sequence of the path of faith for each believer in Christ.

5. The successive rituals of the Hebrew Marriage ceremony.

These patterns tell the same story in different ways; they have the same rhythm and sequence. Every consecutive link in the chain of each pattern can be linked to the link in the other patterns.

Therefore, these patterns can be used to test the Biblical reality of our theology. If we don't agree with something, we may wonder why what we reject is still confirmed in all five patterns? We are called to search out things, to test our own perceptions and keep what is biblically (not theologically) good.

## The Challenge

Is it not clear that as we can expect the Bridegroom in our generation, so we have hope for the future? But there is work to be done, the Bride has 'tapestries' to make! He that overcomes will be clothed in white raiment **as a result** of the Grace we have received at the New Covenantal Pesach. This is the loving response of the Bride to the One who first loved her, seeking first His Kingdom and its righteousness.

# Chapter Seven

# GOD THINKS
# IN COVENANTS

## Introduction

The first ketubah covenant happened when the Bride and Bridegroom entered the Ketubah at Mount Horeb. There they were bound together in a holy, exclusive, unbreakable, unchangeable relationship before the marriage ceremony. Eventually, Israel became unfaithful.[1] For new covenant believers of Israel and the Gentiles, the Ketubah that was given at the Seder meal becomes effective when we are born again, after which our earthly life of faith should reflect the marriage ceremony. The best is yet to come!

## A Covenant is not a Testament

A Testament is like a Will by which a person gives rights on their death, sometimes dependent upon some conditions being met. While a Testament is unilateral, a Covenant is bilateral in that it gives shape to an ongoing *relationship with mutual obligations* on both sides. If a relationship between the same parties and their descendants is renewed, the old covenant between these parties is renewed.

## Why Did God Enter into a Covenant with a Nation?

There is evidence of man-made covenants more than 4,000 years ago. They were between equal partners or between stronger and weaker partners in which the stronger offered protection in return for loyalty and service. It must have seemed strange to surrounding nations that the people of Israel had made a Covenant with an invisible God. Today it may seem equally foolish to the world that believers are in Covenant with an invisible God![2]

In the Book of Deuteronomy we see the structure of the Covenant:

1. **The Introduction**. The place, the time, & the participants are named. **1:1-5. 2.**

2. **Historic Preamble.** The reason for the Covenant. **1:6-4.**

---

1 Jer. 3.
2 1 Cor 1:18.

3. **Conditions.** The commandments to be obeyed to get God's blessing. **5-8.**

4. **Archiving.** Where the text is written down and where kept. **27:2-3.**

5. **Consequences: Blessings and Curses.** The result of good and bad behaviour! **28.**

6. **Witnesses.** Heaven and Earth are the witnesses! **39:19.**

### The Reason for the Covenant

Do we recognise our position in the Covenant made by God with every individual, saved by faith in Christ Jesus? God is not there to help us achieve our own goals of prosperity & success, but to be glorified in us as He empowers us to be His instruments. As Israel of old, we have a Covenant responsibility to learn God's instructions and to pass His Word on to our children.[1]

### A New or Renewed Covenant?

God has made promises in successive Covenants to fulfil His plan.

*'So God heard their groaning, and God remembered His Covenant with Abraham, with Isaac and with Jacob. And God looked upon the children of Israel and God acknowledged them'.*[2]

Despite their disobedience, God's Covenant with them was eternal.[3]

The early Church believed that the Jews were dismissed and disowned by God. The New Covenant, even though the Hebrew word means 'restoration', has replaced both the Old Covenant. The church has not understood that by the Cross God has reconciled Jew and Gentile into one new man.[4] Through this New Covenant God called the believers from

---

1  Deut. 6.
2  Ex. 2:24.
3  Judg. 2:1.
4  Eph. 2:11-16.

the Gentiles to be fellow-heirs and fellow-citizens.[5] Just think about this addition "fellow".

## The Testament and Price Mechanism

Being the weak one, we have entered a bilateral Covenant with the Strong One and that requires responsibility and action on both sides. But there is danger in the belief that Christians are in a unilateral relationship with God 'Who is there to bless us'. The cost of discipleship is often reduced to fill Churches who end up with a prosperity Gospel of all take and no give. We are warned of the likely lukewarm outcome in the Laodicean Church who thought they were rich but were in God's sight wretched, poor, miserable, blind and naked.[6]

God does not want us to stop after our deliverance and justification. Every Biblical pattern shows the need for the testing during the desert journey to deepen our discipleship as we prepare for the Marriage Covenant. And the Word of God and the Holy Spirit is there to equip and guide us.

## Four Types of Covenants

There are four types of Covenants in the Old Testament that are all embedded in the Hebrew wedding ritual. Four types of covenant, with a reason. They give us an insight that being once justified by the blood of the Lamb does not automatically qualify us to attend the Wedding of the Lamb. The four **consecutive** Covenants[7] are:

1. The Blood Covenant.

2. The Salt Covenant.

3. The Sandal Covenant.

4. The Marriage Covenant.

---

5  Eph. 2:19,3:6.
6  Rev. 3:17.
7  We highly recommend reading "Lost in Translation, rediscovering the Hebrew roots of our Faith", John Klein & Adam Spears, 2007.

### The Blood Covenant

When Adam & Eve broke their marriage covenant with God, they were divorced. But God immediately began His plan to rebuild His relationship with mankind. Later, Moses sprinkled the blood of bulls on the people and spoke, *'of the blood covenant which the Lord made with you'*.[1]

An important feature of the blood covenant is that it is to be renewed[2] and it marked the recipient as a slave – not a popular concept when we aim for 'self-fulfilment![3] But Paul died daily by denying himself for the cause of Christ.[4] Spurgeon wrote, *'The saints of the early Church considered themselves joyfully the absolute property of Christ, bought and paid for by Him.'* The Hebrew Bride rejoiced that she had become the Bridegroom's own, longing to do His will. It is the same for us.

### The Salt Covenant

The Salt Covenant between two parties is for ever. Each participant pours his salt into a vessel and it is mixed. The Covenant could only be broken if the salt was re-separated - which was impossible. When God visited Abraham they broke bread as a sign of the salt covenant that is dedicated to **friendship**. God called Abraham His friend, although he still remained a slave from the blood covenant.[5] Nowadays believers prefer to be friends of God rather than servant-slaves. A salt covenant meant loyalty even unto death. Jesus gave up His life – will we give up ours?

### The Sandal Covenant

The Sandal Covenant is about **'inheritance'.** The Hebrew meaning of 'heir' meant that you took good care of your father's property to grow into a mature heir. Old sandals were held on the ground by a stone to mark the limits of one's inheritance. As an example, the transfer of Elimelech's inheritance to Boaz was sealed by the exchange of sandals.

---

1   Ex. 24:8.
2   1 Cor. 11:25.
3   Luke 17:10.
4   1 Cor. 15:31.
5   Gen. 18:1-15.

Today God wants to enter into a sandal covenant with his people to bestow upon them a great inheritance.[6]

Sadly many are like the rich young ruler who was not yet ready to enter a deep relationship and to give all to God. God is always seeking this, but we may be challenged to make a decision that goes against our wishes before we can move to a deeper level of intimacy. David chose God's will by not slaying Saul. Although David committed a very serious sin later, he was still a man after God's heart. Jesus washed His disciples' feet as an example of the humility needed for them to move from being friends to heirs. True servant leaders must have humility to be God's stewards, now and in the age to come.

### The Marriage Covenant

The highest covenant is the **Marriage Covenant**. Adam and Eve ruled over creation as heirs with intimacy and friendship with their Creator. God longs for believers, His servant-slaves, dedicated friends and heirs, to make progress during their earthly lives. But do we first want to obey Him as a slave in the **Blood Covenant**? Do we want to sacrifice our lives as His friends in the **Salt Covenant**? Will we break free from our goals and possessions and become true heirs of all He gives to follow Him in a **Sandal Covenant?**

| Type | Relationship |
|------|-------------|
| Blood Covenant | Master - slave (servant) |
| Salt Covenant | Friend |
| Sandal Covenant | Father - Son / Heir |
| Marriage Covenant | Full spiritual unity |

---

6  Eph. 1:18.

## The Essence of the Covenants

We are called to go through spiritual development as servant-slaves in the Blood Covenant, as dedicated friends in the Salt Covenant, as trustworthy heirs in the Sandal Covenant, growing one day into full spiritual unity in the Marriage Covenant. New life can only emerge when believers die to self so that God can invest His gifts in them to enable them to walk as Jesus walked.[1] Sadly many will miss their inheritance because they want to stay in their comfort zone and seek their own prosperity first. Unsurrendered human strength is often the problem. How can we walk with God in newness of life if we will not die with Him first by denying ourselves, taking up our cross and following Him? Would we rather remain babies on the carpet or grow up in Christ? Do we want to work out our salvation and persevere in running the race? Only then will we have the full white linen dress of the Bride.

## The Four Covenants in the Wedding Ceremony

This last covenant represents the final and full recovery that God has planned since the fall of man. Let us look back at the process. Abraham has sent his servant to find a wife for his son; the relationship of the bride and bridegroom has been revealed in the Song of Solomon; Jesus has told His disciples that He is going to prepare a place for them in His Father's house.

The *ketubah* has been entered into by Jesus Christ since His blood as the Passover Lamb was shed for us. Now believers are encouraged to prepare themselves by moving forward through the discipleship challenges of the salt and sandal covenants before the Bridegroom comes for His Bride for the wedding ceremony. Some may think they are rich but the Lord may tell them that they are lukewarm and naked.[2] How to be overcomers and make progress is illustrated as well in the four cups of wine in the marriage ritual.

---

1  1 John 2:6.
2  Rev. 3:14-22.

**Four Marriage Cups Symbolize four Covenants**

The four successive covenants reflect four cups of wine during the wedding process. The first cup is the **Cup of Sanctification** that symbolizes the blood covenant that sets aside the two families to become one big family. This first cup between the Bride and the heavenly Bridegroom is taken by all believers redeemed by His blood. Unfortunately this grace does not always lead to great dedication to Him.

The second cup is the **Cup of Dedication** that refers to the salt covenant. The negotiations take place over a meal; the bride's father wants to be sure the bridegroom can support her; the bridegroom's father wants to be sure the bride has the right character, as the Heavenly Father seeks a Bride without spot or wrinkle. When negotiations are completed, a second cup of wine is taken by the bride and bridegroom and their respective fathers committing themselves to be 'eternal' friends.

The third cup is the **Cup of Inheritance** taken by the bride and bridegroom, as also by Jesus, after the Seder meal had ended. Thus cup symbolizes that the groom's inheritance is now shared. This cup also reflects the third sandal covenant and underlines that the inheritance is established **before** the Great Wedding has taken place. If believers are unwilling to leave everything behind, to be crucified with Christ, to rise to newness of life and be obedient to His Spirit, they will tend to become lukewarm and complacent. Eventually their faith can be shipwrecked.

**The Fourth Cup of Praise** is only taken by the bride and bridegroom on the wedding day. Jesus referred to this cup when He said that He would not drink of this cup until the Kingdom of God had come.[3] Soon, when the Body of Christ of all generations has been raptured, the Bride and Bridegroom will drink the Fourth Cup, the cup of praise.

---

3  Luke 22:18.

99

## Many Are Called – Few Are Chosen?

We may wonder what Jesus meant by these words?[1] All believers are called to deepen their relationship with Christ but could it refer to the fact that many don't want to give up their freedom or suffer the consequences – they want to keep a bit of the world? Jesus said that His yoke was easy and His burden was light. While this is true when we allow His Spirit to work out His plan in us and receive all we need from Him, **it is up to us to choose how big an inheritance we will enjoy in heaven.**

## Why Continued Cleansing?

Continuous cleansing is a picture of the heart attitude of the Bride who has fallen in love with the Bridegroom and wants to present herself to Him without spot or wrinkle.[2] Being a redeemed friend is not good enough for her. With all her heart, soul, mind and strength she strives for the highest relationship with her Bridegroom. It takes time and many tribulations to conquer with Him. Abraham learned obedience through suffering and testing, as did Joseph, Moses and David. May this last generation also strive to be a spotless Bride.

## An Urgent Call to the Church: Watch and Pray!

We hope that this concise edition of Wake Up! will have touched your heart and that it will help the Church to be vigilant - even to wake up! We repeat that we are not calling for Judaization because there is no longer Jew nor Greek in the context of salvation, but we do believe that our Hebrew heritage is very relevant for Christians today. We pray that readers will have their faith strengthened to become one new man in Christ. As God said to Daniel: *'Go thy way, Daniel, for these things remain hidden and sealed until the end time. Many will purify and sanctify themselves, but the wicked shall do wickedly; and none of the wicked shall understand, but the wise shall understand.'*[3]

*Let us pray that* He helps us to understand and that *we will be among them.*

---

1   Matt. 22:14.
2   Dan. 12:10.
3   Dan. 12:9-10.

This **concise edition** is a summary of the book Wake Up!, God's Prophetic Calendar in Timelines and Feasts. The unabridged version contains 560 pages of in-depth information and more than 1700 footnotes for further study on these subjects. Buying that book also gives entrance to the Wake Up! library, where you can download additional Bible studies and an additional free chapter of 100 pages in e-book format.

Please visit www.wakeup.community for more information and subscribe to the free newsletter.

**NOTES**